EDEXCEL A-LEVEL/AS RELIGIOUS STUDIES

PAPER 3 NEW TESTAMENT STUDIES

3   INTERPRETING THE TEXT

D1744635

Published independently by Tinderspark Press
© Jonathan Rowe 2018

CONTENTS

ABOUT THIS BOOK

This book offers advice for teachers and students approaching Edexcel AS or A-Level Religious Studies, Paper 3 (New Testament Studies). It concentrates on **Topic 3 (Interpreting the text and issues of relationship, purpose & audience)**.

The other topics are:

1 **Social, historical & religious context of the New Testament**

2 **Texts & interpretation of the Person of Jesus**

Together with this one, these books cover the AS course or Year 1 of the A-Level; the remaining books cover the topics in Year 2 of the A-Level.

4 **Ways of interpreting the scripture**

5 **Texts and interpretation: the Kingdom of God, conflict, the death and resurrection of Jesus**

6 **Scientific and historical-critical challenges, ethical living and the works of scholars**

> Text that is indented and shaded like this is a quotation from a scholar or from the Bible. Candidates should use some of these quotations in their exam responses.

Text in this typeface and boxed represents the author's comments, observations and reflections. Such texts are not intended to guide candidates in writing exam answers.

INTERPRETING THE TEXTS

What's this topic about?

How did the New Testament Gospels come to be written? Who wrote them and who was the intended audience? What were they originally trying to say. These questions are addressed in this topic.

INTERPRETING THE TEXT

This topic looks at the **Synoptic Problem** (including **proto-Gospels**, the **priority of Mark**, **Q source**, **2-source and 4-source solutions**) as well as **source criticism**, **form criticism** and **redaction criticism**

THE PURPOSE & AUTHORSHIP OF THE FOURTH GOSPEL

This topic looks at different theories about John's Gospel, including **purpose** (including **spiritual Gospel**, **life in his Name**, **Christ**, **Son of God**, **fulfilling Scripture** and **conversion**) and **authorship**. The key scholars are **Raymond E. Brown** and **C.H. Dodd**.

Before you go any further...

... there are some things you need to know.

THE EARLIEST DOCUMENTS

Jesus wrote no books and none of his followers wrote down his sayings or doings during his lifetime. Everything we know about Jesus was written by someone else, a believer living and writing in the years after Jesus' crucifixion (in 30 CE or 33 CE). This means all the New Testament writers view Jesus in the light of the Resurrection.

> *This is an important point. The Gospels are written by people who believe Jesus has been raised from the dead. This has changed their view of him from whatever they believed about him during his Ministry in the late 20s and early 30s CE.*

The earliest Christians seem to believe that the end of the world was imminent. This means that they too did not write down their recollections of Jesus 'for posterity'. They didn't think there was going to *be* any 'posterity'. The earliest Christian documents we have are the **epistles** (letters) of **Paul**. Throughout the 50s CE, Paul founded Christian churches in Turkey and Greece and wrote letters to his congregations, settling disputes and encouraging their faith. However, Paul never knew Jesus during Jesus' lifetime and only mentions the most basic details of Jesus' life and death (that Jesus was betrayed and crucified, that he had twelve Disciples).

The Gospels were written later, when the generation of Christians who had known Jesus personally started to die. They realised they would need a record of who Jesus was to pass onto a new generations of Christians who had not known Jesus in life - possibly Christians who had never been to Galilee or Judea and knew little or nothing about Judaism.

> *But remember: the Gospels are not just biographies of Jesus. They are written to pass on beliefs about Jesus: that he is the **Messiah**, the **Son of God** and the Saviour of the world.*

The traditional explanation of the Gospels is that they were written *independently* by people closely connected to the historical Jesus:

- **Matthew** and **John** were written by Jesus' actual Disciples, Matthew Levi the tax-collector and John son of Zebedee; Matthew was perhaps written in Antioch where there was a large Jewish population, John perhaps in Ephesus.

- **Mark** was written by the secretary of Jesus' chief Disciple, Peter; since Peter was executed in Rome, this Gospel is supposed to have been written there

- **Luke** was written by Paul's traveling companion, a Greek doctor and Christian convert who met with Peter and the other Disciples; it is thought to have been written in Greece, where Paul founded his churches

Traditionally, all the Gospels were written in the 60s CE, before the Jewish Revolt of 67-74 CE and the destruction of the Temple (Jesus predicts this destruction in the Gospels). Modern scholarship is **secular** in philosophy and does not assume that miracles happen. Secular scholars date the Gospels *after* the Jewish Revolt (which is why Jesus can "predict" the destruction of the Temple - it was actually in the past when the Gospels were written).

Mark's Gospel (68-70 CE, Rome?)

Most scholars now regard **Mark** as the earliest Gospel (this is the theory of **Markan Priority**). Mark emphasises that Christians should expect persecution by Jewish leaders as well as *"governors and kings"* (**Mark 13: 9**) and this probably refers to the Christians being blamed by the Emperor Nero for the fire in Rome in 64 CE. There are several prophecies in Mark about the Temple being destroyed, but the author doesn't seem to know that this has actually happened (which would date Mark no later than 70 CE). Mark explains Jewish customs for his readers (e.g. **Mark 7: 3-4**) which suggests it was written for a church of Gentile converts to Christianity rather than Jewish Christians.

Matthew's Gospel (c.85 CE, Antioch?)

Early scholars used to suppose **Matthew** to be the earliest Gospel, which is why it comes first in the New Testament. This is because Matthew is a very 'Jewish' Gospel: it does not explain Jewish customs the way Mark does, it uses proof-texts from the Old Testament to support its view of Jesus as the Messiah, it shows a good knowledge of 1st century Palestine and a respect for the Jewish Law (e.g. **Matthew 5: 18-19**). Because Matthew refers to Jesus being famous *"throughout all Syria"* (**Matthew 4: 24**), scholars suggest that the Gospel was written for a group of Jewish Christians who escaped the destruction of the Jewish War and moved to Syria, probably to Antioch which had a large community of Jewish Christians.

The Gospel doesn't name its author but early tradition identifies the author as Matthew the Tax Collector from Capernaum who was recruited by Jesus to be one of his Twelves Disciples (**Matthew 9: 9-13**). However, the author does not identify himself as Matthew or write as if he is an eyewitness to the events in Jesus' life.

Luke's Gospel (c.85 CE, Greece?)

Luke is usually regarded as the last of the Synoptic Gospels to be written. It does not claim to be an eyewitness account but instead introduces itself as a report gathered from people who *were* eyewitnesses (**Luke 1: 1-4**). It is written in a good standard of Greek for an educated audience but it only has a hazy understanding of the geography of Palestine. writes about some specific details of the Roman siege of Jerusalem in 70 CE, dating it later than this. Luke has a strong focus on the relevance of Christianity to Gentiles and Jesus' moral teachings; it is sometimes called the 'Gospel of Compassion'. Luke also tries to present Jesus as a philosopher-figure - someone the Roman Empire would find respectable and non-threatening.

John's Gospel (90-100 CE, Ephesus?)

John's Gospel has always been viewed as the last Gospel to be written. It describes Jesus' enemies as "*the Jews*" and seems to come from a time when Christians were ceasing to view themselves as Jewish; it also has a 'high Christology' and regards Jesus as the **Word of God made Flesh**. It refers to Christians being expelled from Synagogues, which took place in the 80s-90s CE. John's Gospel is written in a 'backward-looking' style that refers to the events in Jesus' lifetime as having happened some time ago. However, it has a much more accurate knowledge of the geography of pre-70 CE Jerusalem than the other Gospels. This means some parts of John's Gospel might go back to original eyewitnesses.

All the dates above are speculations. If you read around you will find some Christian books and websites arguing for earlier dates. For example, some would date Luke to the early 60s because Luke doesn't seem to be aware of Paul and Peter dying in Rome during Nero's persecutions. These Christians regard descriptions of the Temple being destroyed as miraculous predictions of a <u>future</u> event rather than recollections of a <u>past</u> event. Your beliefs about miracles will influence how you date these Gospels.

Although John's Gospel is (probably) the latest in terms of composition, it's the earliest in terms of physical evidence. The oldest example of a Gospel yet discovered is the **Rylands Library Papyrus P52**. This fragment of papyrus (an ancient form of paper) was discovered in an Egyptian market in 1920. It contains a fragment from **John 18** on the front and back: the scene where Pontius Pilate asks Jesus, "*Are you the King of the Jews?*" It has been dated to the early 2nd century CE.

THE NEW TESTAMENT CANON... AND THE REST

Matthew, **Mark**, **Luke** and **John** are the canonical Gospels. A 'canon' is an official list. There are non-canonical Gospels that aren't officially recognised and weren't included in the Bible. Sometimes they are called the APOCRYPHA (which is Greek for "hidden things").

These 'apocryphal' or 'non-canonical' Gospels were popular with some churches in the early Christian centuries, but came to be seen as deviant or inauthentic. We know about some of them because early Christian writers mention them (usually with hostility).

- **The Gospel of the Ebionites:** This group of Jewish Christians kept their own Gospel which presented Jesus as a vegetarian prophet; unfortunately, no copies have survived

Some of these Gospels were thought to be lost but copies have been discovered by archaeologists:

- **The Gospel of Thomas:** This is a 'sayings' Gospel the consists only of quotes from Jesus but no story; many of these sayings are very odd and it contains some unusual Parables (such as the whacky Parable of the Assassin)

- **The Gospel of Peter:** This Gospel is violently anti-Jewish, contains fantastical miracles and presents the Jewish king Herod Antipas, rather than the Roman governor Pontius Pilate, as ordering Jesus' execution

- **The Gospel of Judas:** Not written by Judas, but about him; this Gospel presents Judas positively, not as a betrayer but as being ordered by Jesus to hand him over to the authorities

The canonical set of four Gospels (**Matthew**, **Mark**, **Luke** and **John** - the *Tetramorph* or 'set of four' in Greek) are mentioned by **Irenaeus of Lyon** in 180 CE which shows they were informally accepted by Christian leaders early on. By about 400 CE, **Augustine of Hippo** regards the canon as complete and accepted by everyone. So why did these Gospels not make it into the canon?

- Some offer unusual views of Jesus that don't fit with standard Christian beliefs - for example, Jesus arranging for his own betrayal in the Gospel of Judas

- Some belonged to minority Christian sects that faded from history - such as the Ebionites who tried to keep their Jewish roots

- Some were viewed as of late composition and not authentic - such as the Gospel of Peter which has lots of blatantly unhistorical events

However, some Gospels were forced 'underground'. The **Gospel of Thomas** seems to have been suppressed by the Bishop in Egypt in the 4th century CE. Its owners buried it in a sealed pot and it lay undiscovered for over 1500 years until it was accidentally dug up by Muslim farmers in 1945. These books are known as the **Nag Hammadi Library** (after the town where they were found).

Be cautious about what you read about the Nag Hammadi Library. There's no evidence that the Gospel of Thomas was widely popular with Christians or dates back as early as the canonical Gospels. But it is interesting to read a different presentation of Jesus.

TOPIC 3.1 INTERPRETING THE TEXT

The Exam expects you to be familiar with the so-called **Synoptic Problem** and how scholars have interpreted the Gospels through different forms of 'criticism' ('criticism' here doesn't mean attacking the Gospels: it means analysing them in different ways).

Christianity After Jesus

None of the books in the New Testament is written by Jesus. As far as we know, Jesus never wrote down any of his teachings. The New Testament texts were written by Christian believers living in the decades after Jesus, people who passionately believed that Jesus had been raised from the dead and was no longer – or perhaps, had never been – an ordinary human being.

Some scholars refer to these people as the 'primitive' Christians – but 'primitive' in the sense of 'coming first' rather than being savage or basic. The primitive Christians experienced some influential events in the 1st century CE:

33 CE	Jesus is crucified in Jerusalem. In the weeks that follow, his Disciples report encountering him raised to life.
34 CE	One early Christian **Stephen** is stoned to death by a Jewish mob when he describes a vision of Jesus as the Son of Man enthroned in Heaven beside God (**Acts 6: 54-60**).
35-50 CE	The Christian movement spreads among Jews but also attracts Gentile converts. These Gentiles are largely recruited by **Paul** a former **Pharisee** who once persecuted Christians himself but has now become one
50s-60s CE	The Gentile converts pose a problem: do they have to become Jews and follow the Jewish **Law** (including circumcision for the men)? or does the Law no longer apply to Christians? Opinions are divided with Paul arguing against the Law but many of Jesus' original Disciples (perhaps including **Peter**) wanting to continue following it.
64 CE	The Emperor Nero blames Christians for the fire in Rome and puts them to death in gruesome ways. Paul and Peter both die in this persecution.
67 CE	The Jewish Revolt throws off the **Roman occupation**. For a while the **Zealots** take control of Jerusalem and Christians became even more unwelcome, with many moving to Syria.
70 CE	The Romans invade Jerusalem and destroy the Temple, bringing an end to the **Sadducees** and **Essenes** too. Judaism is left without a leadership or a centre of worship.
70s-80s CE	Judaism reforms itself, with the **Pharisees** taking over leadership and the local Synagogues becoming the centre of worship and authority.
90 CE	The **Council of Jamnia** formally expels Christians from the Synagogues.
90s CE +	No longer considered to be Jewish by the Roman authorities, Christians are expected to worship the gods of Rome and the Roman Emperor himself. When they refuse they are arrested and sometimes tortured and executed.

During this period, the Christians preserved memories of Jesus as part of an ORAL TRADITION – stories and teachings being passed on by word-of-mouth and shared when Christians gathered together in worship (the Jewish Christians at Synagogues at first, the Gentile Christians at each other's homes). Paul's **epistles** (letters) from the 50s CE give us some insight into this; we know the Christians gathered for a 'Love Feast' where bread and wine were shared (the **EUCHARIST**).

Dating of the Gospels

The traditional belief is that the Gospels were written in the late 50s or early 60s, before the persecutions by Nero and before the destruction of the Temple in 70 CE. The Gospels feature predictions that the Temple **will be** destroyed, but don't state that this has in fact happened. The **Book of Acts**, which is a sort of sequel to Luke's Gospel, does not seem to be aware that Peter and Paul have been executed.

If the Gospels were written this early, they really could be the work of the people they are traditionally linked to: **Matthew** the tax-collector who joined Jesus Disciples, **Mark** the secretary of Peter, **Luke** the companion of Paul and **John** the Disciple of Jesus. The Gospels would contain authentic eyewitness accounts of the things Jesus said and dead.

Today there is a lot of disagreement between scholars over this. Many think that the Gospels were written **after** 70 CE, possibly right at the end of the 1st century CE. They were **not** written by eyewitnesses but by later Christians who had received an oral tradition about what Jesus said and did – an oral tradition that might have deviated pretty far from the historical facts in the intervening decades. This means there is a huge amount of interest in the 'oral period' when Christianity was taking shape: the decades after Jesus' lifetime but before the Gospels were written down.

- Did oral tradition faithfully preserve Jesus' historic behaviour, words and teachings? This is the view of many Catholic and conservative Protestant scholars?

- Did oral tradition massively distort Jesus' behaviour, words and teachings, possibly attributing to Jesus many beliefs that have no basis in fact? This is the claim of more liberal or modernist scholars.

There's a similar disagreement about Christology (beliefs about who Jesus is). Low Christology views Jesus as a human being EXALTED (raised up, promoted) by God to a supernatural state' high Christology views Jesus as a divine being who has been INARNATED in human form.

- Did the low Christology emerge earlier in the oral period and the high Christology develop later?

- Does either type of Christology actually date back to Jesus' lifetime: are these beliefs Jesus had about himself and taught his followers or did they develop later?

The Quest for the Historical Jesus

19th and 20th century scholarship pursued what **Albert Schweitzer** called *"the quest for the historical Jesus"* (1906). Many scholars focus on the distinction between that **Martin Kahler** terms *"the Jesus of history and the Christ of faith"* (1892). The 'Historical Jesus' was a 1st century Jewish preacher who was executed by the Romans; the 'Christ of faith' is a cosmic being worshiped by millions and composed of ideas developed long after the historical Jesus died.

In fact, Kahler meant something different by his phrase, but the idea has stuck and someone has to get credit for it!

Jesus of History	Christ of Faith
Jesus of Nazareth was a genuine historical figure: a Palestinian Jew of two thousand years ago whose life, death and message profoundly influenced the people of his day. Even those who deny Jesus was the Son of God do not deny his existence. They may even approve of his life and message and find them worth studying, alongside other great religious leaders. These people are reflecting upon the historical Jesus.	Christians do not believe that Jesus became divine through his Resurrection; they believe that he was divine and one with God from the beginning of time. They believe that, in the person of Jesus, God became one of the human race in order to redeem us from our sin. When Christ was raised from the dead, he became our Lord and Saviour. For them, the Jesus of history is the same thing as the Christ of faith: Jesus was and is both human and divine.

The idea of the 'historical Jesus' first appears in the writings of **Hermann Reimarus** (1694-1768) whose posthumously published *Wolfenbüttel Fragments* put forward the idea that the historical Jesus was very different from the 'Christ' who was invented by his later followers.

Reimarus proposes that Jesus was a Jewish prophet who had no intention of founding a separate religion, but who got involved with a failed rebellion against the Romans and was executed for it. Jesus' followers stole his body to fake his resurrection from the dead.

Reimarus' ideas are pretty hard-core even by the standards of Internet trolls. You will encounter his theory in more detail if you go on to **Topic 4 (Ways of Interpreting the Scriptures)**

Some scholars propose that the historical Jesus can be discussed, analysed and re-imagined quite separately from the Christ of faith - that the two have almost nothing to do with each other. For example, some scholars have proposed that Jesus was a Zealot or a Cynic philosopher or an unremarkable Jewish exorcist but they still worship Christ as a **symbol** of the love of God.

However, not everyone finds this idea easy to grasp and, for many, separating the historical Jesus from the Christ of faith leads to the *loss* of faith: if Jesus is nobody special in history, then Christ is just an idea his followers invented after he died, not someone who reveals God *"in Grace and Truth"*.

The scholars who are prepared to re-interpret Jesus in fairly radical ways that make sense to modern readers are the MODERNISTS. The scholars who want to conserve the traditional idea of Jesus as a preacher, miracle-worker and Messiah are the CONSERVATIVES.

Sometimes the modernists are termed liberals and the conservatives are termed traditionalists.

This cartoon (from a traditionalist viewpoint) shows modernist Bible critics descending into darkness and atheism. The symbolism is straight out of John's Gospel!

In the 1980s, a group of 50 Bible scholars formed the **Jesus Seminar** to discuss, research and publish ideas about the historical Jesus. The Jesus Seminar codes passages in red that Jesus probably did say or do, in pink if its possible Jesus said or did them, grey if it's unlikely and black if Jesus almost certainly didn't really say or do these things. The Jesus Seminar is a modernist project and works on the assumption that miracles don't happen and that Jesus was an ordinary human and not a supernatural being.

This is the source of the conflict today between conservative/traditionalist and liberal/modernist Christian thinkers. For conservatives, the historical Jesus *is* the Christ of faith: he's a supernatural person who preformed miracles and predicted his own crucifixion and Resurrection. Liberals question these things and are prepared to admit that most of what we believe about Christ was invented decades or centuries after the death of Jesus.

THE SYNOPTIC PROBLEM

The Synoptic 'Problem' isn't really a problem in the same way that the **Problem of Evil** is a problem for believers. It's more of a puzzle that scholars have proposed different answers for over the years.

What is the Synoptic Problem?

Christians have always recognised a similarity between the three 'Synoptic' Gospels (**Matthew**, **Mark** and **Luke**). 'Synoptic' means 'seen together' and when passages from the Synoptic Gospels are placed side by side they can be seen to be remarkably similar. Sometimes they are word-for-word the same, but at other times they differ slightly, with one Gospel adding words or phrases or the other Gospel omitting them.

Here is an example: the miracle of the **Feeding of the 5000**, which is described in all 3 Synoptic Gospels and in **John**. This translation tries to capture the phrasing of the original Greek and the word used for 'fish' is noted:

SYNOPTIC GOSPELS			NON-SYNOPTIC
Matt 14:19-20	**Mark 6:41-42**	**Luke 9:16-17**	**John 6:11-12**
Taking the five loaves and the two fish (*ichthus*), looking up into heaven he blessed, and breaking, gave to the disciples the loaves, and the disciples to the crowds. And all ate and were satisfied.	And taking the five loaves and the two fish (*ichthus*), looking up into heaven, he blessed and he broke up the bread, and was giving to the disciples in order that they set before them, and the two fish he distributed to all. And all ate and were satisfied.	But taking the five loaves and the two fish (*ichthus*), looking up into heaven, he blessed them and he broke up, and was giving to the disciples to set before the crowd. And they ate and were satisfied.	Thus Jesus took the loaves, and giving thanks, he distributed to the ones reclining; similarly also, whatever they desired from the fish (*opsarion*). And when they are full, he says to this disciples, "Gather the remaining pieces in order that nothing be lost."

> *You can see how the Synoptics use the same phrasing and the same Greek word for fish (ichthus, meaning the actual animal) whereas John uses different phrasing and a different word for fish (opsarion, meaning fishy food, like a kipper)*

Agreement in Wording

When Matthew, Mark and Luke describe the same episode, on average they share 50% of the same Greek words used to describe it (in contrast, they share 10% of the same words with John). Some passages are even more similar than that: when they introduce John the Baptist, the Matthew and Mark share 90% of their Greek words.

> *John wore clothing made of camel's hair* (trichon kamelou), *with a leather belt* (zonen dermatinen) *round his waist [and] he ate locusts* (akrides) *and wild honey* (meli agrion) - **Mark 1: 6 and Matthew 3: 4**

> *Remember that Jesus and his disciples spoke Aramaic, not Greek. How likely is it that Matthew and Mark would use <u>exactly</u> the same words and phrases in Greek to translate Aramaic?*

Parenthetical Material

'Parenthesis' means 'brackets' - when a text adds a comment for the reader in brackets to make a point clearer (like this). All the Gospels contain parenthetical material; in fact, John's Gospel contains the most. However, the parenthetical material in the Synoptics is usually identical. Parenthesis is something used in writing, not in speech so this feature can't be due to the Gospel-writers being eyewitnesses to the same speeches or conversations. Here's an example:

> *(Let the reader understand)* - **Mark 13:14 and Matthew 24: 15**

> *This parenthetical statement is deliberately addressed to a "reader" - not a 'listener' - so it's clearly been composed by the author, not some earlier eyewitness. What are the odds Matthew and Mark would use the <u>exact same phrase</u> to clarify the <u>exact same point</u> in the story?*

Luke's Prologue

Luke's Gospel begins by explicitly claiming to have taken material from earlier sources:

> *just as they were handed down to us by those who from the first were eyewitnesses* - **Luke 1: 2**

> *Luke is admitting right at the start that he's using material that was 'handed down' and not creating a Gospel "from scratch"*

Matthew 9: 9-13	Mark 2: 13-17	Luke 5: 27-32
	[13] Once again Jesus went out beside the lake. A large crowd came to him, and he began to teach them.	[27] After this, Jesus went out
[9] As Jesus went on from there,	[14] As he walked along,	
he saw a man named Matthew sitting at the tax collector's booth. 'Follow me,' he told him, and Matthew got up and followed him.	he saw Levi son of Alphaeus sitting at the tax collector's booth. 'Follow me,' Jesus told him, and Levi got up and followed him.	and saw a tax collector by the name of Levi sitting at his tax booth. 'Follow me,' Jesus said to him, [28] and Levi got up, left everything and followed him.
[10] While Jesus was having dinner at Matthew's house, many tax collectors and sinners came and ate with him and his disciples.	[15] While Jesus was having dinner at Levi's house, many tax collectors and sinners were eating with him and his disciples, for there were many who followed him.	[29] Then Levi held a great banquet for Jesus at his house, and a large crowd of tax collectors and others were eating with them.
[11] When the Pharisees saw this,	[16] When the teachers of the law who were Pharisees saw him eating with the sinners and tax collectors,	[30] But the Pharisees and the teachers of the law who belonged to their sect
they asked his disciples, 'Why does your teacher eat with tax collectors and sinners?'	they asked his disciples: 'Why does he eat with tax collectors and sinners?'	complained to his disciples, 'Why do you eat and drink with tax collectors and sinners?'
[12] On hearing this,	[17] On hearing this,	
Jesus said, 'It is not the healthy who need a doctor, but those who are ill.	Jesus said to them, 'It is not the healthy who need a doctor, but those who are ill.	[31] Jesus answered them, 'It is not the healthy who need a doctor, but those who are ill.
[13] But go and learn what this means: "I desire mercy, not sacrifice."		
For I have not come to call the righteous, but sinners.'	I have not come to call the righteous, but sinners.	[32] I have not come to call the righteous, but sinners to repentance.'

This episode, describing Jesus calling Matthew (also called Levi) to be his disciple, shows how similar the Synoptic Gospels can be.

Implications: independent versions of the same story?

Some Christians argue that Matthew, Mark and Luke all independently came up with their Gospels, recording an 'oral tradition' (story passed on by word-of-mouth) that had been handed down to them. They explain the Synoptic similarities like this:

- The Gospel-writers were all describing the same historical events so obviously they describe them in the same ways

- The Gospel-writers were all inspired by the Holy Spirit to write in the same way

The first solution is historically naive. For one thing, even though the Gospel-writers describe some things in the same way, they describe other things in different ways. Why would they do that? John's Gospel doesn't match the wording of the Synoptics (John's wording is 92% unique). Does this mean that John's Gospel describes completely different events?

> *This argument would imply that Jesus was crucified twice: once the way the Synoptic Gospels describe it and once the way John's Gospel describes it. But that's absurd. Clearly, they're describing the <u>same</u> crucifixion, so we need a different explanation for the similarity in the way the Synoptics describe things.*

The idea of divine inspiration faces the same problems: why would the Holy Spirit inspire the Gospel-writers to use the same language and describe the same details some times - but not others? Why would the Holy Spirit inspire John to describe things differently - or is John's Gospel not inspired by the Holy Spirit after all?

Implications: interdependence or a proto-Gospel?

A popular solution is that the Synoptic Gospels are **interdependent**: they have all copied from each other. Church tradition states that Matthew was the first Gospel to be written and that Mark and Luke copied passages from Matthew (with Mark cutting out details and Luke adding more in). This is the theory of MATTHEAN PRIORITY.

A different solution to the Synoptic Problem would be the existence of another **Proto-Gospel** (p18). This is an early original version of the Gospel story that the Synoptics are copying passages from. If they are all using the same proto-Gospel, that would explain their similarities. If John's Gospel does not make use of the proto-Gospel for its material, that would explain John's differences in language and style.

The problem is that no trace of a proto-Gospel has been discovered by archaeologists and there is no mention of a proto-Gospel by any of the ancient Christian writers like **Irenaeus**, **Jerome** and **Augustine**, who all describe Matthew, Mark and Luke as the earliest Gospels known.

Is the Synoptic Problem really a problem for believing in the Bible?

YES

NO

Christians claim the Gospels are "*inspired*" texts - they are revelation from God. The Synoptic Problem suggests they have a more straightforward origin: they are copied from a lost **Proto-Gospel**.

The Gospels are still "*inspired*" even if parts are copied. Luke's Gospel clearly states it has used sources in its prologue. The Synoptic Gospels probably copied from each other or Mark and Luke copied Matthew.

If there was a lost Proto-Gospel, then it was closer to the historical Jesus than the Gospels we now have. That makes the Bible unreliable. It shows that books of the New Testament are ordinary literary texts, products of human error and human judgment.

If the New Testament writers were inspired by the Holy Spirit, then you would expect coherence and unity in their writings and this is what you find. There's no evidence for any 'proto-Gospel'; it's more likely the Synoptic Gospels products of are different eyewitnesses.

Proto-Gospels

One solution to the **Synoptic Problem** would be the existence of a lost Gospel - a **proto-Gospel** ('earliest Gospel') that the Synoptic Gospels all copy from. Some scholars use the term ur-Gospel instead of proto-Gospel.

*"Proto-gospel" is an odd term for the exam board to use. If you type 'proto-gospel' into a search engine, you won't find much except links to a text called the **Protoevangelion of James**. This is a late-2nd century birth narrative based on **Matthew** in which Mary and Jesus hide from Herod's soldiers. It's <u>not</u> a proto-gospel and it's got <u>nothing</u> to do with this topic so please ignore it.*

A proto-Gospel would be an <mark>early written version of the Gospels</mark> (like a PROTOTYPE or 'first attempt') that the Synoptic Gospels copy from. The idea is that **Matthew**, **Mark** and **Luke** all had this proto-Gospel in front of them when they wrote their Gospel accounts; they copied some of it but they made changes, adding details in or ignoring passages that didn't suit them.

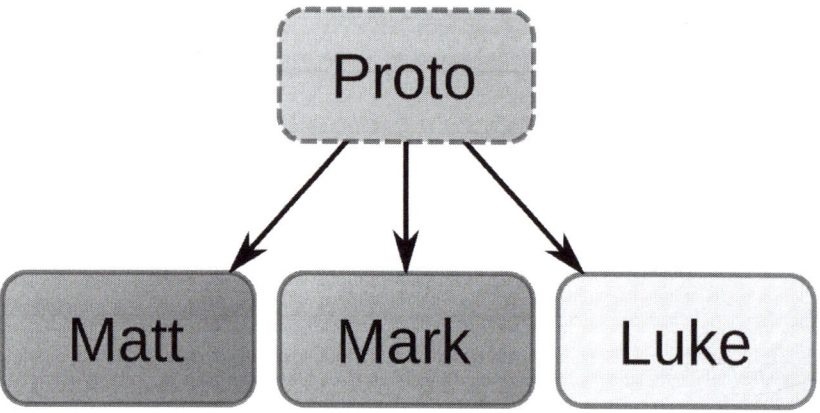

- The proto-Gospel is written in Aramaic originally, but the Gospel-writers perhaps had a Greek translation

- The proto-Gospel probably includes just the sayings (*logia*) of Jesus and the Gospel-writers added in situations and settings

- The proto-Gospel represents the original preaching (*kerygma*) of Jesus and his Disciples before it was altered by later generations of Christians

The strongest evidence for this is that Luke's Prologue (**Luke 1: 1-4**) clearly states that people before him have "*drawn up an account*" of Jesus' Ministry and that these people were "*eyewitnesses*" but that he is merely "*writing an orderly account*" of this source.

The biggest weakness is that there is no reference to this proto-Gospel in any of the earliest Christian writers. Around 130 CE, **Marcion of Sinope** lists his personal 'canon' of New Testament scripture, but doesn't mention the proto-Gospel (he prefers Luke). **Irenaeus of Lyon** refers to the canonical four Gospels (the *Tetramorph*) in 180 CE, again with no mention of any proto-Gospel.

Early writers mention several Christian texts that are lost to us now (such as the *Gospel of the Ebionites*) and some that were lost for centuries but have been discovered by archaeologists (such as the *Gospel of Thomas*) but they never mention the proto-Gospel or anything that sounds like it.

The Gospel of Thomas: a proto-Gospel?

The long-lost *Gospel of Thomas* was discovered at **Nag Hammadi** in 1945. Scholars suggested that it could be the missing proto-Gospel. In its favour, Thomas does consist entirely of *logia* (sayings of Jesus) with no narrative or story to give them context. About half of these *logia* appear in the Synoptic Gospels too.

Thomas might have inspired John's Gospel more indirectly. **Elaine Pagels** points out that John seems to have passages that specifically refute *logia* in Thomas, as if John's Gospel was written to prove Thomas wrong. For example, a *logion* in Thomas says that the light of God is born from within, but John says that the world does not recognise the **True Light**. Thomas himself appears as a character in John's Gospel: he doubts Jesus' Resurrection and is proved wrong.

On the other hand, the *Gospel of Thomas* doesn't seem to be early enough to be a proto-Gospel. The copy discovered at Nag Hammadi dates from the 4th century CE and is translated from an original from the 2nd century CE.

Bart Ehrman points out that Thomas lacks the main characteristic of the earliest Christian writing: APOCALYPTICISM or the belief that the world is about to come to an end. It seems more likely that Thomas is based on the Synoptics rather than that the Synoptics are based on Thomas.

Could Matthew be the proto-Gospel?

The early church writers believed **Matthew** to be the first Gospel written, with Mark and Luke copying passages from Matthew. The theory that Matthew is the proto-Gospel is called **MATTHEAN PRIORITY**. This is also known as the **AUGUSTINIAN HYPOTHESIS** because it was proposed by **Augustine of Hippo**.

According to this view, Matthew was one of Jesus' Twelve Disciples and wrote his Gospel in Aramaic or Hebrew. It was translated into Greek and this was the version used by Mark and **Luke** to write their Gospels, with Mark abbreviating Matthew to create a shorter Gospel (but adding in some material based on the preaching of Peter) and Luke using Matthew and Mark to create an expanded Gospel.

This theory makes sense and explains why the earliest Christian writers regard Matthew as the earliest Gospel and why there's no mention of an earlier proto-Gospel. This is sill the view taken by the Catholic Church.

Augustinian hypothesis

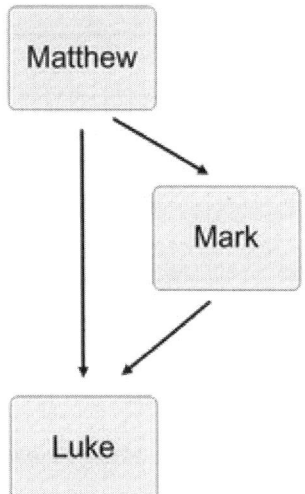

The main problem with this theory is that Mark misses out so much material from Matthew: for example

- the Virgin Birth
- the Lord's Prayer
- the Sermon on the Mount

These are such important passages, it's hard to see why Mark would not include this material if he knew about it from Matthew. The earliest versions of Mark do not even contain descriptions of the Resurrection: why would Mark not copy *that* from Matthew? This has led to the alternative theory of **Markan Priority** (p22) in which Mark is the proto-Gospel instead.

Implications

If there is a lost **proto-Gospel** out there (or if Thomas is that proto-Gospel), then the New Testament is fundamentally unreliable. This is because the proto-Gospel represents a much more authentic version of Jesus' real sayings and teachings, which have been added to and perhaps distorted by the Synoptic Gospels.

For example, there is no **APOCALYPTIC** element in Thomas - no teachings about the imminent end of the world. The apocalyptic element is certainly present in the canonical Gospels. There's also no crucifixion in Thomas. If Thomas is the proto-Gospel, then Jesus never taught that the world was going to end or that he was going to be crucified. Instead, his followers added these teaching to their Gospels after Jesus' crucifixion, creating a religion very different from the one Jesus taught.

However, the development of Christian ideas seems to be the opposite way round. As time goes on, Christian writing becomes less and less apocalyptic and more reconciled to the fact that the world is not going to end and Christ is not coming back straight away. It seems more likely that a proto-Gospel would be apocalyptic rather than the Gospel-writers adding apocalyptic fantasies to a proto-Gospel that didn't share these concerns.

The existence of proto-Gospels is important for the **4-Source Solution** (p28) to the **Synoptic Problem**.

Does the theory of a proto-Gospel solve the Synoptic Problem?

YES	NO
The Synoptic Gospels must have gotten their testimony about Jesus from somewhere and the similarities between them suggest that they didn't all come up with it independently. A lost proto-Gospel would explain the similarity in language and structure between the Synoptic Gospels.	No proto-Gospel that matches the Synoptics has been discovered: it's pure theory. The *Gospel of Thomas* doesn't fit the bill (lack of apocalyptic themes or crucifixion) and Matthew can't be the proto-Gospel that Mark uses because too much stuff is missed out.
A proto-Gospel is a 'stepping stone' between the word-of-mouth preaching of Jesus and his Disciples (called the *kerygma*) and the eventual composition of the Synoptic Gospels. Since the Gospels were written decades after Jesus' time, the authors would need a 'source' to base their stories on.	Liberal scholars date the Gospels late in the 1st century CE but traditionalists date them much earlier. If the Synoptics are independent eyewitness accounts of the events of Jesus' life, they don't require an intermediate 'source'. There was no need for proto-Gospels because actual Gospels were written straight away.

The Priority of Mark

For centuries, Matthew was regarded as the earliest Gospel. This was the view of **Irenaeus of Lyon** and **Clement of Alexandria** in the 2nd century CE and it was supported by detailed argument by **Augustine of Hippo** (the Augustinian Hypothesis). However, since the 18th century, the majority of Bible scholars have come round to the view that Mark, not Matthew, is the earliest Gospel. This is the theory of **Markan Priority** (with 'priority' meaning 'coming first').

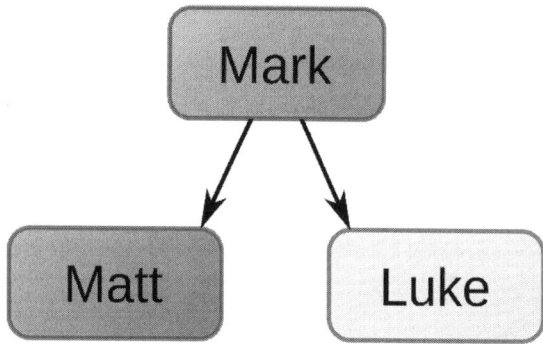

There are several problems with the Augustinian Hypothesis (that **Mark** is an abridged or shortened version of **Matthew**):

1. Mark does not feature several passages that are very important to Christians: the Virgin Birth, the Lord's Prayer, the Sermon on the Mount and (in its earliest versions) appearances by the Risen Christ after the Resurrection. Since these passages are important in Matthew, it's hard to explain why Mark would leave them out if Mark was copying Matthew.

2. Mark has very poor Greek grammar and uses a lot of slang words, whereas Matthew and Luke are written in quite correct Greek. It's hard to explain why Mark would take Matthew's good Greek and deliberately mess it up

3. Similarly, Mark contains a number of Aramaic words and expressions that aren't in Matthew. For example, **Mark 7: 11** uses the Aramaic word "*corban*" to mean a ritual dedicated to God. Why would Mark deliberately add Aramaic expressions into Matthew's narrative (then explain them in Greek)?

However, if Mark is the first Gospel and was copied by Matthew and Luke, these puzzles disappear:

1. Mark missed out these passages because he didn't know about them; Matthew and Luke add them in to 'fill out' the story Mark tells

2. It makes sense that Matthew and Luke would correct Mark's bad Greek

3. Mark uses Aramaic expressions because he's translating from the original Aramaic that Jesus and his Disciples spoke; Matthew and Luke are writing for a Greek-speaking audience that wouldn't understand these expressions, so they take them out

One of the most powerful arguments for Markan Priority is the presence of HARD READINGS in Mark. These are passages which describe Jesus in unflattering ways or which seem to go against later Christian beliefs about Jesus. In every case, Matthew and Luke cut out or tone down these passages, making them less difficult for Christians to accept.

> *[Jesus] looked around at them in anger* - **Mark 3: 5**

This suggests Jesus had a temper. Matthew completely misses out this verse, but Luke changes it to something less problematic:

> *[Jesus] looked around at them all* - **Luke 6: 10**

> *Jesus getting angry goes against the Christian image of of "gentle Jesus, meek and mild". Mark was writing when there was still a memory of the historical Jesus who did get angry sometimes; Matthew and Luke describe a less historical but more perfect person who never loses his cool*

A similar argument is based on CHRISTOLOGY (beliefs about Jesus' relationship to God). Mark seems to have a 'low Christology' or what **Bart Ehrman** calls an 'Exaltation Christology'. This is the belief that Jesus is human being who is EXALTED (raised up, promoted) by God. Mark begins his story with Jesus being baptized by John the Baptist (**Mark 1: 9-11**) and suggests that this is the moment when Jesus becomes **God's Son**.

Whereas Matthew and Luke present Jesus as being the **Son of God** from the moment of his conception. Most scholars think a low Christology comes earlier in Christian tradition than a high Christology (**John**, which has the highest Christology of all - an INCARNATION CHRISTOLOGY - is the latest Gospel).

Implications

If these arguments are correct (and the majority of Bible scholars think they are), then Mark is the earliest Gospel - perhaps the **proto-Gospel** - and Matthew and Luke both had copies of Mark in front of them when they wrote their Gospels. Matthew kept a lot of Mark's text (90% of it) and Luke kept rather less (about 50%).

This also makes sense of Luke's Prologue, which claims to "*write an orderly account*", from an earlier source:

> *Many have undertaken to draw up an account of the things that have been fulfilled among us* - **Luke 1: 1**

This passage could refer to Mark and perhaps the **Q-Source (p25)** and **Special Luke** (p28).

Does the theory of Markan Priority make the Bible more trustworthy?

YES	NO
Mark was the secretary/translator of **Peter**, the leader of Jesus' Twelve Disciples. Therefore, his Gospel is based on the best possible eyewitness. That's why Mark uses Aramaic expressions and preserves some 'hard readings' - it's authentic history.	By presenting Matthew and Luke as simply copying chunks of Mark and making their own changes, this theory presents the Bible as a creation of flawed humans rather than a set of independent eyewitnesses inspired by the Holy Spirit.
Markan Priority is essential for the **2-Source** and **4-Source** solutions to the **Synoptic Problem**. It explains the similarity between the Gospels and (if we take the **Q-Source** into account) the differences as well.	These solutions break up the unity and coherence of the Gospels by presenting them as 'jigsaws' or 'collages' made up of different sources stitched together, rather than independent eyewitnesses.

The *Q*-Source

If we accept the theory of **Markan Priority** (p22), the **Synoptic Problem** does not completely go away. There is still a lot of material shared by **Matthew** and **Luke** which isn't in **Mark**. This is explained by the theory of the **Q-Source**.

There are 230 passages where Matthew and Luke share close (almost word-for-word) texts, but which aren't in Mark. These include:

- **Jesus being tempted by the Devil:** Matthew 4: 1-11 and Luke 4: 1-13

- **The Beatitudes (Sermon on the Mount):** Matthew 5: 3-12 and Luke 6: 20-23

- **The Lord's Prayer:** Matthew 6: 9-13 and Luke 11: 1-4

- **Many Parables, such as the Lost Sheep:** Matthew 18: 12-14 and Luke 15: 1-7

A theory to explain this is that Matthew and Luke both had access to the same source- another **proto-Gospel** that contained these passages. In the 20th century, this mysterious source was termed **Q** (short for *Quelle*, which is German for 'source').

> *So the 'Q-source' is really the 'source-source'.*
> *And while we're at it, it's S-O-U-R-C-E, not SAUCE.*
>
> *It's not something you put on a chip butty.*

Q would have been a collection of sayings (*logia*) of Jesus - although the story of Jesus' temptation and the healing of the Centurion's Servant seem to be from *Q* too, so perhaps it had narratives in it as well as sayings. There's a lot of debate about whether *Q* was originally written down or whether it was a memorised list of *logia* that was recited in churches. Luke seems to preserve more of the original order of *Q* than Matthew, who spreads the various *logia* throughout his Gospel.

No copy of **Q** has ever been discovered. More baffling, there's no mention of **Q** existing by any of the early church writers who discuss the background of the Gospels. However, there is this tantalizing quote from **Papias of Hieropolis** (125 CE):

> *Matthew compiled the* logia *of the Lord in a Hebrew manner of speech, and everyone translated them as well he could* - **Papias of Hieropolis**

This used to confuse scholars because Matthew's Gospel was originally written in Greek, not Hebrew or Aramaic. But perhaps this is a reference to the ***original*** Matthew the Disciple creating **Q** in Aramaic, which the Gospelists Matthew and Luke (we don't know their real names) 'translated as well as they could' into Greek.

This would make sense of Luke's Prologue where he describes how:

> *Many have undertaken to draw up an account of the things that have been fulfilled among us* - **Luke 1: 1**

Luke admits to basing his Gospel on previous sources, so *Q* could be what he is referring to here.

Implications

The **Q-Source Hypothesis** is accepted by the majority of Bible scholars, but not by everyone. The lack of any clear reference to **Q** in ancient Christian writings is puzzling, because a book containing the authentic *logia* (sayings) of Jesus would have been a treasured possession of early Christians. However, maybe once **Q** was incorporated into Matthew and Luke's Gospels, Christian readers preferred them to a dry list of sayings (because the Gospels give the sayings a context and dramatize them) and the original collection was forgotten about.

> The **Q-hypothesis** has been developed into the **2-Source** and **4-Source** solutions to the *Synoptic Problem*.

Some fundamentalist Christians object to the **Q**-hypothesis. They believe that the Gospels are eyewitness accounts written by the original **Matthew** (a Disciple), **Mark** (Peter's secretary) and **Luke** (Paul's traveling companion). The **Q**-hypothesis suggests that Luke and Matthew's Gospels were actually written by people who had no personal link to Jesus or his Disciples. Instead, they cobbled their Gospels together from a list of old sayings, perhaps inventing situations to give these sayings a context. Such Christians are suspicious that the **Q**-hypothesis is just another attempt by atheists to make the Bible look like a flawed human document rather than scripture inspired by God.

Does the Q-hypothesis make the Bible more trustworthy?

YES	NO
The theory of the **Q**-Source provides a link from Gospels written in the 80s CE back to the events of Jesus' lifetime. Matthew and Luke are written *after* the destruction of the Temple in the Jewish Revolt but draw upon materials like **Q** from *before* that important event.	There is no evidence for **Q** - either physical evidence (no copies exist) or literary evidence (no ancient writers ever refer to it; instead they refer to the four canonical Gospels being the earliest accounts). **Q** is a theory that supports a late dating of the Gospels preferred by atheists.
No copies of **Q** are known - but then no copies of the *Gospel of Thomas* were known until the Nag Hammadi Library was discovered in 1945. Thomas is another 'sayings Gospel' - a collection of *logia*. This makes the existence of **Q** more plausible, as do references by Papias and in Luke's Prologue.	If the canonical Gospels are what they have always been claimed to be - independent eyewitness accounts of Jesus' ministry, crucifixion and Resurrection - then there's no need for **Q**. If the Gospels were written in the 60s CE then there's no need for a 'sayings Gospel' since this is within the lifetime of the historical Matthew, Mark and Luke.

SOLUTIONS TO THE SYNOPTIC PROBLEM

The ideas of **Markan Priority** (p22) and the **Q-source** (p25) have been widely accepted, among liberal scholars at least. This has led to two popular solutions to the **Synoptic Problem**.

The 2-Source Solution

This solution was proposed in the 19th century. It states that **Matthew** and **Luke** both used **Mark** and the **Q-source** to write their Gospels, with Matthew relying more heavily on Mark and Luke on **Q**. Matthew and Luke then improve upon this material (e.g. improving on Mark's Greek and removing Aramaic phrases) and they both add context and background to the material from **Q** (which is just a collection of *logia* or sayings).

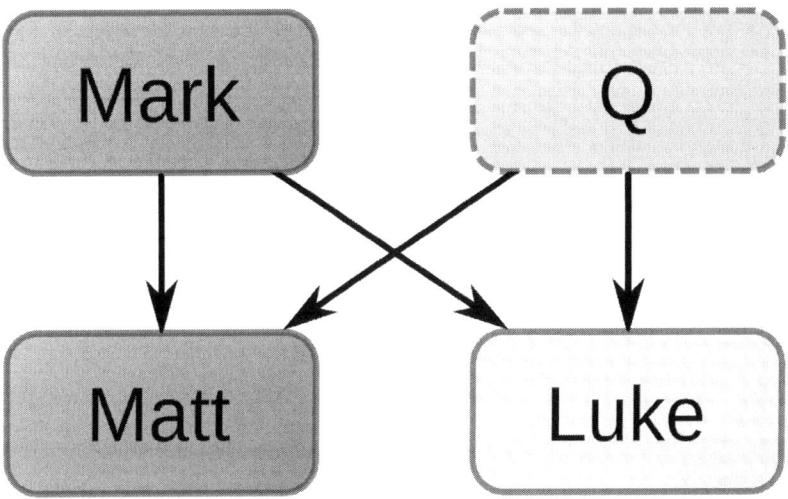

We can see Matthew and Luke improving on Mark in their use of terminology. Mark refers to **Herod Antipas**, the ruler of Galilee, as a "king" (*basileus*), which isn't strictly correct. Luke changes this to Antipas' correct title of "*tetrarch*". However, Matthew seems to get tired of correcting Mark on this and after starting off calling Herod Antipas a *tetrarch* he lapses back into Mark's incorrect title of *basileus*. This reveals Mark's material 'showing through' Matthew's Gospel.

The 4-Source Solution

Burnett Streeter (1924) suggested this improvement on the 2-Source Solution. Streeter suggests that, as well as drawing upon Mark and **Q**, Matthew and Luke made use of two **proto-Gospels**, (p18) referred to as Special Matthew (or **M**, Matthew's unique source, which Streeter thinks comes from Jerusalem) and Special Luke (or **L**, Luke's unique material, which Streeter thinks comes from Antioch in Syria).

This means there are a total of 4 sources being used: Mark, **Q**, **M** and **L**. Matthew did not have access to **L** and Luke did not have access to **M** but both used Mark and **Q**.

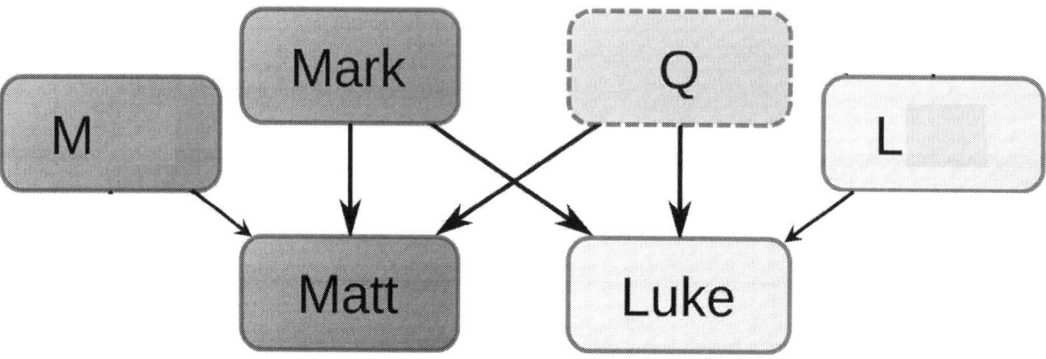

The 4SS is very popular among scholars who date Matthew and Luke to the 80s CE and propose that they were ***not*** written by actual Disciples of Jesus or Paul. The 4SS explains how people living far away from Jerusalem and Galilee and long after the crucifixion of Jesus could get their information about what happened. For this reason, the 4SS is unpopular with fundamentalist Christians because they argue that Matthew and Luke were written at the same time as Mark, in the 60s CE, by actual Disciples who were eyewitnesses and therefore didn't need 'sources'.

Implications

These solutions depend on the existence of **Q** and we have no physical evidence for this text and no direct reference to it in early Christian writings. Fundamentalist Christians often attack these solutions by denying the existence of **Q** and claiming that Matthew and Luke are eyewitnesses who don't needed sources. These solutions also depend on **Markan Priority** (p22), which is widely accepted but some scholars (especially Catholics) continue to propose versions of the Augustinian Hypothesis that Matthew is the earliest Gospel, copied by Mark and Luke.

Both of these solutions have a problem with MINOR AGREEMENTS between Matthew and Luke. Matthew and Luke are supposed to have been written independently, without knowing each other and without access to each other's Special Sources (**M** and **L**). However, there are passages where they use the same words to describe events that aren't in Mark or **Q**. A famous example is the scene where the Roman soldiers mock Jesus. They blindfold him, hit him and then say:

> *"Prophesy! Who hit you?"* - **Matthew 26: 68 and Luke 22: 64**

> *Some scholars explain this by saying that Luke **did** have access to Matthew (this would be the 3-source solution or 3SS). Others suggest that this passage could be in a different version of Mark from the one we have today (but there's no evidence for that).*

Despite this, the 2SS and 4SS are the most popular solutions to the **Synoptic Problem** as the moment. There are even fundamentalist Christians who are prepared to accept the 2SS, because it explains the material shared between Mark, Matthew and Luke so well. The 4SS is more controversial, because it presents Matthew and Luke as 'copying and pasting' different documents together rather than writing accounts of what they themselves experienced.

An important fact in the popularity of the 4SS is disbelief in miracles and prophecy: many modern scholars think Matthew and Luke must have been written **after** the destruction of the Temple in 70 CE because they describe Jesus predicting it... however, fundamentalist Christians argue that Jesus **really did** predict this through the power of prophecy, so the Gospels date from **before** 70 CE. The persuasiveness of these solutions depends to a large extent on your own beliefs about **miracles** and the **Person of Jesus**.

Do the 2- and 4- Source Solutions really solve the Synoptic Problem?

YES	NO
The 2SS and 4SS are both elegant solutions: they don't involve bringing in extra complications; in philosophical terminology, they are PARSIMONIOUS. They also have real explanatory power (they show exactly **how** the Gospels were put together).	These solutions depend on unproven theories. For example, the existence of the **Q-source** is essential to both of them, but **Q** has never been discovered and is not mentioned by early writers. **Markan Priority** also goes against early tradition which is that Matthew is the first Gospel.
The 4SS has a particular benefit of explaining how the Gospel writers late in the 1st century CE could have access to information from the time of Jesus' ministry in the 20s and 30s CE: they made use of **proto-Gospels** (Special Matthew and Special Luke).	This is only an advantage if you refuse to accept that Jesus could have miraculously predicted the destruction of Jerusalem in 70 CE. But if Jesus was the **Son of God** then he **COULD** prophesy and so the Gospels are from the 50s or 60s CE, written by eyewitnesses who don't need 'sources'.

THEORIES OF BIBLICAL CRITICISM

Source Criticism

If you've studied the pages on the **Synoptic Problem** (p13) and its **2- or 4-Source Solutions** (p27), then you will have seen Source Criticism in action.

Source Criticism is an approach to New Testament Studies that tries to determine the sources used to develop the final form of the Biblical text. A Source Critics asks, **"Where did the author get this information? What previous documents or word-of-mouth traditions contributed to this?"**

This type of criticism treats Bible texts as human documents that have been created in the same way as other biographies, histories or legends. It ignores the role of **revelation** or the Holy Spirit *'inspiring'* writers. Source Criticism does not treat the Bible as inerrant (without mistakes) - on the contrary, it looks for mistakes or contradictions as indications that material from two different sources may be present. For example, Mark incorrectly refers to Herod Antipas as a "king" but Luke and Matthew correct this to "*tetrarch*"; on the occasions when Matthew refers to Antipas as "king" that's an indication he is using Mark as a source.

Source Criticism was originally applied to non-religious texts, for example the classical literature of Ancient Greece. In the 18th century, **Jean Astruc** took the techniques that Source Critics had used on Homer's *Iliad* and applied it to the Old Testament, demonstrating that several different sources had been used to create the **Book of Genesis**.

Since then, Source Criticism has identified the **Synoptic Problem** as involving different sources being used by Mathew, Mark and Luke. Source Critics propose **solutions** involving **proto-Gospels** (p18), **Markan Priority** (p22) and the **Q-source** (p25).

In a nutshell: Source Criticism looks at texts as jigsaw puzzles or collages made up of various 'bits' that originally came from somewhere else; it tries to identify the components of a text and trace their origin back to earlier sources.

Implications

Source Criticism has secular (non-religious) assumptions:

- The Bible is a collection of human documents, not divinely inspired ones

- The Bible contains errors and contradictions

- The Bible's books were assembled through copying and editing earlier sources rather than being eyewitness testimonies

New Testament Source Criticism is also linked to the late dating of the Gospels. Traditionalists who believe the Gospels are eyewitness accounts date them to the 50s or 60s CE and treat the predictions about the destruction of Jerusalem in 70 CE as a miraculous prophecy; Source Critics treat these prophesies as "wisdom with hindsight" being written after 70 CE, making it look like Jesus predicted things that he didn't. Source Criticism explains how people living long after Jesus' time could use earlier sources to write Gospels that seem (on the face of it) to read like eyewitness accounts.

Traditionalists reject these assumptions: for them, the Bible is divinely inspired, inerrant (without mistakes) and the product of eyewitnesses who saw Jesus' miracles with their own eyes. They often view Source Critics as trying to undermine religious faith with their theories.

Is Source Criticism helpful for interpreting the New Yestament?

YES	NO
Source Criticism is elegant (leaving few remaining questions) and has great explanatory power. It offers a view of how the Gospels were composed that doesn't involve guidance by the Holy Spirit, amazing coincidence in wording or miraculous prophecies.	Source Criticism is a bunch of wild theories that cannot be backed up. None of the 'sources' has been discovered - we have no records of *Q* or any of the so-called proto-Gospels and they are never mentioned by early Christian authors either.
Source Criticism explains the similar material in the Synoptic Gospels by proposing these writers shared the same sources. The alternatives are much harder to believe: that the Gospel-writers were mystically controlled by the Holy Spirit or just coincidentally used the same words to describe things. **Occam's Razor** tells us to prefer the simpler explanation.	Source Criticism often has an agenda: to undermine Christian faith by presenting the Bible as a flawed, human document and break up its unity and coherence into a set of contradictory 'sources' that disagree with each other. Instead of helping, this makes it impossible to interpret the New Testament as relevant to living today; it just becomes another old book.

Form Criticism

Source Criticism (p30) has been around for hundreds of years but **Form Criticism** only developed in the 20th century in the works of a group of German Bible scholars. As with Source Criticism, this new type of criticism was first applied to the Old Testament then moved on to the New Testament later.

Form Criticism tries to go back further than identifying sources. It assumes that the Gospels are made up of **"units"** of text (for example, Parables or miracle stories) and that these 'units' were passed down as part of an **oral (word-of-mouth) tradition** before they were written down in the Gospels. Form Critics try to identify these 'units' within the text, compare them to each other and work out what they *originally* meant before they ended up in the Gospel. These 'units' are called **PERICOPAE** by Form Critics.

The founder of Form Criticism was **Hermann Gunkel** (1918) who used a key phrase to explain how it works: "*Sitz im Leben*", which means "setting in life". This refers to the social context that a 'unit' of text was created in and what it meant to the Christian group that first used it.

Form Critics argue that before the Gospels were written down, there was an **'oral period'** where stories about Jesus and sayings (*logia*) attributed to him were passed around by believers. **Martin Dibelius** (1919) suggests there are at least five FORMS of text in the Gospels:

- **Paradigms** (brief stories presenting Jesus as a role model which may be based on Jesus' IPSISSIMA VERBA or "true words")
- **Tales** (longer miracle stories that are meant to entertain)
- **Myths** (stories which explore a truth but which aren't historical)
- **Legends** (stories which seem to be historical but which present the hero as stereotypically heroic)
- **Exhortations** (wise sayings and teachings)

Form Critics argue that the Gospel-writers pulled together these *pericopae* into an overall story, but often didn't understand the *Sitz im Leben* of the group that had originally told them. This means that some stories get misinterpreted. **Rudolph Bultmann** is a famous Form Critic of the 20th century who argues that stories about Jesus were almost entirely misunderstood by the Gospel-writers and need to be **DE-MYTHOLOGIZED** (stripped of their supernatural details) to get back to their original meaning.

In a nutshell: The Gospels are made up of lots of different units of text all strung together: miracle stories and Parables and wise sayings and memorable stories. These units were all separate *pericopae* back in the oral period before the Gospels were written down, then they got 'fixed in place' in the finished Gospel. Form Criticism tries to unpick these *pericopae* and reconstruct what they originally meant.

Examples of Form Criticism

Paradigm: In **Mark 2: 18-22**, Jesus is questioned about why his Disciples aren't fasting and Jesus answers with famous images of a wedding and wine being poured into new wineskins. This is a paradigm: it's brief and memorable and it emphasizes Jesus' special teachings. **Dibelius** thinks it may preserve an actual thing Jesus said: his *ipsissima verba*. However, the *Sitz im Leben* is that early Christians were trying to workout whether they had to follow the **Jewish Law** or not. This text (which suggests Christians don't have to follow the Law) may have been changed or even invented to support an argument going on in the early years of Christianity.

> *Form critics are very interested in pinning down speeches and actions that might go back to the historical Jesus - but they don't think there are many*

Tale: In **Mark 6: 42-45**, Jesus walks on water. **Dibelius** thinks that the *Sitz im Leben* may have originally been a religious experience for some of Jesus' Disciples but it has been expanded into a miraculous story. Form Critics like Dibelius and (especially) **Bultmann** don't believe in miracles, so they see these tales as exaggerations or fantasies which sometimes get in the way of a moral message that was the original point. For example, Bultmann thinks the **Sign of Feeding the 5000** was originally a message of sharing that got overshadowed by a miracle story.

> *Form criticism does think there are important messages in the Bible - just not the ones traditional Christians find there*

Myth: In **Matthew 4: 1-11**, Jesus fasts in the desert and is tempted by the Devil. This story contains many deep issues about faith, moral choices and evil. Many Christian artists have described it, painted it and dramatised it; **Fyodor Dostoevsky** devotes a wonderful chapter of *The Brothers Karamazov* (1880) to exploring it.

But according to **Dibelius** and **Bultmann**, it didn't happen and is fiction. Bultmann suggests a *Sitz im Leben*, that the early Christians were criticized for worshiping a magician, so they compose this myth to refute that criticism (because it shows Jesus refusing to perform miracles for popularity).

Another *Sitz im Leben* could be that early Christians were encouraged to join the **Zealot** movement but this myth was created to reject that course of action (because Jesus refuses worldly power offered by the Devil).

Legends: Matthew's birth-narrative shows Jesus having a supernatural birth and surviving murder attempts by a jealous rival. Alexander the Great was supposedly conceived when a thunderbolt fell from heaven and made his mother pregnant; Plato was said to be the son of the god Apollo. Hercules was the son of Zeus and a mortal woman and the jealous goddess Hera sent two snakes to kill him in the crib.

From a Form Criticism perspective, Matthew is providing Jesus with the sort of birth-narrative that all the great heroes of Greek and Roman history and mythology have. Dibelius calls this the Law of Biographical Analogy (which means, your hero must have a biography similar to the existing heroes in your world). **Bultmann** (of course) goes even further, arguing that Jesus' Resurrection is a Legend too, because lots of heroes in pagan mythology die and come back to life (notably Adonis, Dionysus and Osiris).

> *Form criticism treats Christianity as "just another myth"*

Exhortations: These are wise proverbs, often fairly general in character, that don't have any particular context. Some may not even be Jesus' own teachings. For example, the Jewish teacher **Hillel the Elder** (died 10 CE) summarised the Jewish **Law** with this phrase:

> *What is hateful to you, do not do to your fellow: this is the whole Torah* - **Hillel the Elder**

This is known as the **GOLDEN RULE** in Ethics and Jesus repeats it:

> *Do to others what you would have them do to you, for this sums up the Law and the Prophets* - **Matthew 7: 12**

Form Critics suggest that this *pericope* might originally have been a Jewish exhortation that got added to Jesus' teachings during the 'oral period' then found its way into the Bible. The *Sitz im Leben* would be a community of Jewish Christians familiar with Hillel's teaching who wanted to present Jesus as being just as wise as Hillel.

> *Notice how form critics often deny Jesus' originality or special-ness by focusing on what he shares with (or borrows from) others. Christians point out that Jesus' version of the Golden Rule goes further than Hillel's: Hillel tells you what **not** to do but Jesus tells us what **to** do*

Implications

Source Criticism has some implications that traditional Christians are uncomfortable with, but Form Criticism is much more hostile to traditional beliefs about Jesus and the New Testament - especially **Rudolph Bultmann**'s version of Form Criticism.

Form Criticism presents most passages in the Gospels as fictional or at least wildly exaggerated - and sometimes as originally referring to someone other than Jesus! Form Criticism casts a lot of doubt on whether it is possible to reconstruct a 'historical Jesus' from the Gospels. It presents most of the beliefs about Jesus as taking shape *after* Jesus' lifetime among Christian communities who were developing myths and legends about their founder.

It also suggests that the Gospel-writers threw these *pericopae* together without understanding the point and purpose of them. Form Critics see it as their job to "get behind" the Bible and reconstruct the original stories about Jesus, which might have been rather different from the versions that appear in the Gospels. The sort of scholars who argue that Jesus was really a **repentant Zealot** (R.F. Brandon) or a **wandering Cynic philosopher** (John Dominic Crossan) are coming from a background of Form Criticism; so too are the scholars (and lazy websites) who argue that Christianity has 'stolen' myths and stories that originally applied to pagan gods like Adonis or Mithras.

Obviously, traditionalist Christians are completely opposed to these interpretations. They argue that Form Criticism is essentially subjective and imaginative; since we have no records of these *pericopae* as they were before the Gospels recorded them, Form Critics are free to imagine anything they like and most of them like to imagine things that diminish the importance of Jesus and undermine Christian faith.

On the other hand, Christians do appreciate some insights from Form Criticism, such as the idea that the **Prologue in John** is a hymn that was original sung when Christians worshiped together. There are different genres in the Gospels and that there have been confusions in the past when readers failed to recognise that a passage like this is really a poem.

Does Form Criticism help us to interpret the New Testament?

YES	NO
Form Criticism recognises that the Gospels are made up of units with different genres: there are myths and legends as well as memories of the actual words of Jesus. Form Criticism helps separate the *IPSISSIMA VERBA* (true words) of the Historical Jesus from the fictional stuff.	Form Criticism goes even further than **Source Criticism** in breaking up the unity and coherence of the Gospels, carving them up into stand-alone units that only meant something to a particular group in the past. This gives the Bible little relevance to today.
The Gospels can be relevant to today, but first they have to be DE-MYTHOLOGIZED. The Gospel-writers misunderstood a lot of the material they used and took supernatural events at face value. When stripped of these supernatural elements, the original preaching (*kerygma*) of Jesus can be found. For example, the **Feeding of the 5000** is really a message about the importance of sharing.	The interpretations Form Critics offer are utterly subjective and reflect their own atheist assumptions and prejudices. They assume that miracles don't happen and that Jesus was just an ordinary moral philosopher, then 'discover' that anything striking about Jesus' teaching or life is really just a commonplace bit of ethical advice. This makes the Bible less interesting and influential, not more.

Redaction Criticism

In some ways, Redaction Criticism is the oldest type of Biblical Criticism because it focuses on what distinctive beliefs and perspectives different Biblical authors bring to their material. For example, it has long been recognised that **Matthew** presents a very Jewish Jesus who **fulfils** Old Testament prophecy, **Luke** presents a compassionate Jesus who is the Saviour of the world and **John** presents Jesus **as the Word made Flesh**.

However, Redaction Criticism has become very influential since the 20th century. It has built on (and largely replaced) **Form Criticism** (p32) as a popular way of interpreting the New Testament.

Like **Source Criticism** (p30), Redaction Criticism regards the Gospels as being composed from various sources available to the Gospel-writer (**Mark, Q, proto-Gospels**). Like **Form Criticism** (p32), Redaction Criticism also acknowledges these sources are composed from 'units' (*pericopae*) that grew out of an oral tradition before they came to be written down. However, the big difference is the importance of the Gospel-writers themselves- this person is an editor or **REDACTOR** of the material they use.

Form Critics like **Rudolph Bultmann** [*left*] tend to present the Gospel-writers as ignorant about the true meaning of the texts they draw upon; Redaction Critics focus on how the Gospel-writers **choose, edit and alter the texts** to suit their own purposes and express their distinctive agenda.

For example, **John**'s use the phrase "*the Jews*" to describe Jesus' enemies (eg in the **Sign of Raising Lazarus**) reveals his own anti-Semitic agenda.

- Redaction Critics look for recurring **MOTIFS** in a text that indicate the writer's priorities. For example, in **Matthew** the proof-texts show his focus on Jesus fulfilling Old Testament prophecy; in **John** the **"I Am" Statements** reveal John's high Christology.

- Redaction Critics compare two different accounts of the same event (eg in the Synoptic Gospels, or comparing **John** with the Synoptics) and focus on what one writer leaves in or takes out (for example, **John** never names Jesus' mother and downplays John the Baptist's role)

- Redaction Critics identify the distinctive vocabulary and style of an author (for example, **Luke** referring to Jesus as "*Lord*" or **John** referring to "*Eternal Life*") and what this reveals about the writer's beliefs

> *When you consider all these examples from earlier in the course, you'll see that you've been 'doing' Redaction Criticism all along*

Redaction Critics tend to use three techniques developed by Form Criticism to explore how the Gospel-writes redact (edit) their texts:

- **Criterion of Multiple Attestation:** If a passage or event appears independently (not copied from the same source), then it's more likely to be historical. For example, all the Gospels describe the crucifixion of Jesus independently of each other.

- **Criterion of Embarrassment:** The Gospel-writers try to remove details that are embarrassing for their beliefs (for example, details that show Jesus to be flawed) but if these details are included it suggests they are historical

- **Criterion of Dissimilarity:** The Gospel-writers often describe Jesus as imitating Jewish themes in the Old Testament or else 'project back' their own Christian practices onto Jesus. If a passage has Jesus behaving in a way that is unlike Jewish practices and also unlike later Christian practices, this 'double dissimilarity' suggests it is historical. A good example would be Jesus forgiving the woman caught in adultery (the *Pericope De Adultera*, **John 8: 1-11**): Jews did not forgive adultery and neither did the early Christians, so this passage is unlikely to be copied from an earlier Jewish source or invented by a later Christian one.

In a nutshell: Redaction Criticism regards the Gospel-writers as careful editors (**redactors**) whose choices of what to leave in, what to leave out and what to change reveal their distinctive beliefs and concerns.

Examples of Redaction Criticism

The Messianic Secret: Wilhelm Wrede is a Redaction Critic that you studied in **Topic 1 (Context of the New Testament)**. He presents **Mark** as a redactor who adds in passages to his Gospel where Jesus demands people keep his Messiah-ship a **secret**. Wrede thinks this reveals Marks agenda which is to present Jesus as the **Messiah** even though Jesus did not claim to be the Messiah in his lifetime.

> *Wrede's theory is largely discredited (for example, by **Morna Hooker**) but it is a good example of Redaction Criticism at work*

John the Baptist: John the Baptist is an important figure in the Gospels. He lives in the desert, wearing animal skins and fasting. He has a huge following and he preaches that Jews should repent their sins; as a sign of this repentance, he baptizes people in the River Jordan. He is executed by Herod Antipas at the time when Jesus began his ministry (perhaps 30-32 CE).

- In **Mark's Gospel**, Jesus comes to be baptized by John at the very start of his ministry. This is when the Holy Spirit descends on Jesus and God's voices declares that Jesus is his Son (**Mark 1: 1-11**).

- In **Matthew**'s version, John also condemns the Pharisees as a "*brood of vipers*". When Jesus comes to be baptized, John is unwilling to baptize him because he recognises that Jesus is greater than him; however, Jesus insists and John obeys (**Matthew 3: 1-20**)

- In **Luke**'s version, John is revealed to be related to Jesus (they are cousins); not only does John condemn the Pharisees but he baptizes publicans and soldiers too; he explicitly tells people he is not the **Messiah (Luke 3: 1-22)**

- In **John's Gospel**, John the Baptist appears in the Prologue: there is no mention of him baptizing Jesus; instead he explains at length that he is not the Messiah; John identifies Jesus as the "*Lamb of God*" who will provide a TRUE baptism with the Holy Spirit and some of his followers leave to follow Jesus instead **(John 1: 1-37)**

This passes the **criterion of multiple attestation**: its in all the Gospels and **Flavius Josephus** describes John baptizing people in his *Jewish Antiquities* (94 CE). The **criterion of embarrassment** makes it likely John really did baptize Jesus (it's embarrassing for the early Christians to admit so they wouldn't make it up) and the **criterion of dissimilarity** adds to idea that this is a historical event.

Redaction criticism can explain the different descriptions in the Gospels:

- **Mark** presents Jesus as a **secret Messiah**, so John does not recognise him as anyone special. Mark also has a 'low Christology' and views Jesus as human so he doesn't see a problem with Jesus needing to be baptized.

- **Matthew** has a higher Christology and does see a problem with Jesus being baptized by John - it implies that John is Jesus' superior. Matthew adds in the exchange between them to make clear that the baptism is just 'for appearances'. He also makes John agree with his own agenda: he represents John as attacking the Pharisees too

- **Luke** has a more universal message and presents John as baptizing the same outsiders that Jesus preaches to. Luke clarifies that John is not the Messiah, which suggests that there were followers of John who thought he *was* the Messiah.

- **John** goes out of his way to make John the Baptist inferior to Jesus: there is no baptizing scene and John the Baptist deliberately explains that he's not the Messiah and that Jesus is. The fact that John's followers join Jesus shows that Jesus replaces John.

Redaction Criticism shows how, as time goes by, the Gospel-writers inflate the status of Jesus and diminish the status of John the Baptist. If there were a rival sect devoted to John the Baptist in the 1st century (perhaps believing that John had been the Messiah, not Jesus), then these passages are Christian propaganda to prove the rivals wrong. The embarrassing detail about Jesus being baptized by John is sidelined then deleted. John is turned into someone who 'prepares the way' for Jesus, not an important religious leader in his own right.

A more controversial theory is that Jesus was actually a **FOLLOWER** of John the Baptist who broke away to form his own group (taking some of John's followers with him). This would definitely be a detail that the Gospel-writers would delete, but if it was well-known then Mark, Matthew and Luke could not avoid mentioning the baptism of Jesus; John, writing much later in the 1st century, could avoid it because all the people who knew the historical Jesus were by then dead.

Implications

Redaction Criticism emphasizes the creative role of the Gospel-writers and encourages readers to consider what the writer is trying to convey by including details or leaving them out. This encourages careful reading of the Gospels, which is a good thing. Unlike **Form Criticism** (p32), it doesn't present the Gospels as a mess of conflicting 'units' or the historical Jesus as irrecoverable. However, it does borrow from Form Criticism a sense of the importance of the social setting (*Sitz im Leben)* that the early Christians operated in. The Gospel-writers are trying to correct or reinforce some issue in their own community in the 1st century and this keeps the historical context in focus.

There are objections to Redaction Criticism. It represents the Gospel-writers as being creative to the point of deception: they delete material that they know is true or else twist it in misleading ways to serve their agenda. This turns the Gospels into propaganda writing rather than truthful accounts. There's no sense that the Gospels are "*inspired*" and they are certainly not eyewitnesses: they are more like pieces of modern journalism with lots of bias.

Traditional Christians will reject this view of the Gospel-writers as untruthful and biased. They regard scripture as being "*inspired by God*".

> *Prophets, though human, spoke from God as they were carried along by the Holy Spirit* - **2 Peter 1: 21**

However, Christians do appreciate some aspects of Redaction Criticism, such as focusing on the different concerns that characterise each of the Gospels and explaining why there are differences between John and the Synoptics or between the way Matthew and Luke use a passage from **Mark** or **Q**. For example, Luke reports Jesus saying "*blessed are the poor*" (**Luke 6: 20**, from the **Q-Source**); Matthew reports this too but alters it slightly to "*blessed are the poor in spirit*" (**Matthew 5: 3**). Both writers interpret Jesus differently: Luke is focused on literal poverty, Matthew on spiritual poverty. This sort of Redaction Criticism gives a fuller picture of the Gospels and Christians do not object to it.

Does Redaction Criticism help us to interpret the New Testament?

YES	NO

If we accept that Matthew and Luke adapt **Mark**, **Q** and their own **special sources**, then Redaction Criticism helps us understand why they leave some things in, take other things out and make the changes they do. It credits the Gospel-writers with being artists with a message rather than just regurgitating sources and oral traditions.

Many Christians reject the idea of the **Q-Source** or **Proto-Gospels**, arguing there's no evidence for these documents existing. Traditionalists view the Gospels as eyewitness accounts of Jesus' life and Resurrection, not the work of editors imposing their own 'slant' on events they never personally saw

There are many puzzling gaps in the Gospels or passages that don't make obvious sense. Redaction Criticism clarifies these passages by looking at the historical context in which the Gospels were written and who their audiences were. It provides the best way of getting back to the 'historical Jesus' behind the 'Christ of faith'.

The puzzling passages in the Gospels should be approached with prayer and humility, not by assuming the Gospel-writers are liars. Most of the historical context Redaction Critics write about is pure speculation and there is a strong atheist agenda in a lot of Redaction Criticism to portray Jesus as an ordinary 'man of his time' rather than the Risen Son of God.

TOPIC 3.2 PURPOSE & AUTHORSHIP OF THE FOURTH GOSPEL

The Exam expects you to be familiar with the so-called Fourth Gospel (**John's Gospel**) and the different theories about who wrote it and why.

John son of Zebedee

This is the traditional author of the Fourth Gospel, one of Jesus' Twelve Disciples. He is the youngest of the Disciples and his older brother James is also one of the Twelve. The two brothers were Galilean fishermen who became followers of John the Baptist, then left to follow Jesus.

According to tradition, John's brother James was the first of the Disciples to be martyred, but John lived to a ripe old age in Ephesus (in modern Turkey) and died in 98 CE. This would make him in the right place and time to write the Fourth Gospel which is named after him (although the Gospel never claims to be written by 'John').

There are three **epistles** (letters) in the New Testament that claim to be written by John. These certainly have similar themes and concerns to the Fourth Gospel and could be written by the same person, but Christian critics have always been rather divided on whether they were written by John son of Zebedee or another Christian called 'John' (it was a very common name).

There is also the **Book of Revelation** which is written by someone called 'John' and is addressed to the Christian churches in Turkey. Tradition says this is the same John, who was sent into exile on the island of Patmos (near Ephesus) by the Romans. However, the language and tone of Revelation is very different from the Fourth Gospel, so scholars doubt it really is the same writer.

Argument for Authorship

19th century scholars used to think the Fourth Gospel was very late 2nd century, so far too late for John son of Zebedee to be the author. However, modern scholars place the date of the Fourth Gospel in the 90s or 100s CE, so possibly within the lifetime of John.

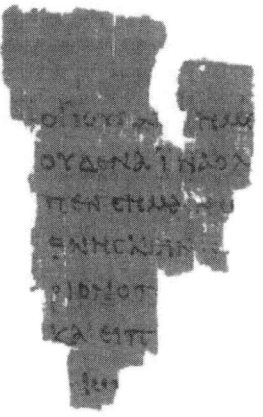

The discovery of **Rylands Library Papyrus P52** confirms this: this ancient manuscript is a fragment of the Fourth Gospel which has been carbon dated to the early 2nd century, proving that the Gospel is not as late as people used to think.

John Robinson, in *The Priority of John* (1984) goes further, arguing that the Fourth Gospel dates from the 60s CE, because it never mentions the destruction of the Temple taking place and shows such detailed knowledge of Judea before the Great Jewish Revolt.

Robinson argues that John son of Zebedee is the Gospel-writer and is in fact the 'other disciple' known to the High Priest who was an eyewitness at Jesus' trial (**John 18: 15-16**).

The main argument against John's authorship is that he was a Galilean peasant fisherman, whereas the Fourth Gospel is written in a good standard of Greek with a knowledge of **Hellenic (Greek) philosophy**. It doesn't seem likely that someone from John's background would write like this. However, in his long life it is possible John could have received a good education and mastered Greek philosophy.

The Beloved Disciple

A mysterious figure appears in the final chapters of the Fourth Gospel, referred to as "*the disciple whom Jesus loved*" or "*the beloved disciple of Jesus*". This person appears 5 times: at Jesus' farewell Discourse, at the foot of the Cross, at the Empty Tomb and 2 times when the Risen Christ appears to the other Disciples; the Fourth Gospel ends claiming that the Beloved Disciple wrote the Gospel down:

> *This is the disciple who testifies to these things and who wrote them down. We know that his testimony is true* - **John 21: 24**

Notice, though, that the author isn't claiming to be the Beloved Disciple: this passage suggests that the Beloved Disciple has died and his followers have written the Fourth Gospel based on the Beloved Disciple's testimony.

So, who is the Beloved Disciple? There are several theories:

- **John son of Zebedee:** This was the view of several early Christian writers. **Polycrates of Ephesus** (d.196 CE) claimed that John was the Beloved Disciple. John son of Zebedee is never mentioned in the Fourth Gospel, so the Beloved Disciple must be him, by a process of elimination. However, the Beloved Disciple only appears in **John 13**, whereas John son of Zebedee was a Disciple right from the beginning.

- **Lazarus:** The Beloved Disciple only makes an appearance after **Lazarus has been raised from the dead**. Lazarus is three times described as the person Jesus "*loved*". This also explains the odd tradition in **John 21: 22-23**, that the Beloved Disciple cannot die until the Second Coming of Christ - if Lazarus really was raised from the dead, people might have thought he was immortal.

- **It's symbolic:** The Beloved Disciple might not be a single person at all, but instead represents believing Christians generally - or the reader in particular. Perhaps YOU, the reader of the Fourth Gospel, are supposed to identify with the Beloved Disciple and "*testify to these things*" yourself by believing in Jesus

The Johannine Community

Raymond E. Brown proposes that the Fourth Gospel wasn't written by a single person: it was a community effort, written in stages, beginning in the 60s CE and not complete until 100 CE. Brown thinks the **Johannine Community** were originally followers of John the Baptist who stayed as part of the Jewish religion right through to the 80s CE. They believed Jesus to be their Messiah.

After the destruction of the Jerusalem Temple, Judaism reorganised itself. In 90 CE, the **Council of Jamnia** set out new rules for Jewish worship and expelling the *minim* (heretics, which included Christians). The Johannine Christians found themselves friendless and despised. They were in danger, because if they refused to worship the Roman gods (and the Emperor) they could be arrested because they were no longer exempted for being Jews. Brown thinks some of them were executed and this produced bitter feelings towards their former Jewish friends.

The Johannine Community had an influx of new members who were converted Samarians (a group that was disliked by the Jews and disliked the Jews in return). This intensified the Community's us-versus-them view of the world. It also helped them survive persecution and develop a very high Christology - a view of Jesus as the **incarnation of God's Word**.

Brown argues that the Fourth Gospel doesn't just report the life and Resurrection of Jesus: it's also an **allegory** for the experiences of the Johannine Community itself:

- The Gospel starts with John the Baptist, because the Community began as followers of John the Baptist; John is presented positively (he recognises that Jesus is the *Light of the World* and the *Lamb of God*) but diminished in status (he does not baptize Jesus, he is not the Messiah)

- Jesus starts his Ministry by cleansing the Temple of money-changers; this comes at the *end* of Jesus' ministry in the Synoptic Gospels but the Fourth Gospel establishes the theme of conflict with the Jews early on

- Jesus visits Samaria and makes converts there (**John 4: 39-42**), representing the ethnic makeup of the Johannine Community of Samarians and former-Jews

- Jesus' **Signs** establish that he is creating a new religion that will separate from Judaism, as with new wine from water, healing the blind man or raising Lazarus; a key breaking point with Judaism is over observing the Sabbath rules, which Jesus ignores.

- The other Christian churches founded by the Apostles are represented by Peter and the Twelve Disciples. The Beloved Disciple is always shown to be closer to Christ than they are: he sits with Jesus at supper, he is at the foot of the Cross, he outruns Peter to get to the Empty Tomb. This represents the Johannine Community being 'ahead' of other Christians at the time with its high Christology.

By viewing the Fourth Gospel in terms of the **Sitz im Leben** *of the Johannine Community in the 80s and 90s CE, Brown is drawing from* **Form Criticism**; *by looking at how the editor (redactor) of the Gospel uses the material to push his own group's agenda, Brown is drawing from* **Redaction Criticism**.

The Structure of the Fourth Gospel

Raymond E. Brown sets out this plan of the Fourth Gospel:

The Prologue (John 1: 1-18)

This is a hymn worshiping the **Logos** that establishes Christ's pre-existence (he existed before the human life of Jesus); it is interspersed with passages where John the Baptist comments on Jesus being the Word of God.

The Book of Signs (John 1: 19 - John 12: 50)

A series of Signs, Discourses and encounters where the Word of God reveals himself to the world but his own people will not accept him. There are **7 Signs** and 7 **"I Am" statements** that explore their meaning. In addition, there is the important meeting between Jesus and Nicodemus where being 'Born Again' is discussed. This section concludes with the final Sign which is the **raising of Lazarus from the dead** and the decision of the Jewish High Priest to execute Jesus.

The Book of Glory (John 13:1 - John 20: 31)

The Word of God reveals his Glory by dying on the Cross and returning to God, the Resurrection and his Ascension to a fully glorified **Eternal Life** that he shares with **believers**. This is the section where the Beloved Disciple appears. If the sections of the Gospel were originally distinct sources, then this might be the source that comes from the Beloved Disciple's eyewitness testimony.

Epilogue (John 21: 1-25)

A series of Resurrection appearances in Galilee and the concluding testimony of the Beloved Disciple. Since the Book of Glory has already come to a very final conclusion, scholars suggest this section was added later (probably after the Beloved Disciple's death).

Brown believes that these sections may have begun as separate **sources** but that the final author of the Gospel **redacted** them together to form a single book.

> *This is a good example of the way **Source Criticism** identifies different sources within a text and **Redaction Criticism** explores how they have been put together by the redactor (editor). The identification of the opening prologue as a 'hymn' is an example of **Form Criticism**. Brown is a Catholic priest, but some Christians would object to breaking the Gospel up like this and insist it should be read as a consistent unity.*

JESUS AS CHRIST

In **John's Gospel**, the 'Book of Signs' concludes with this appeal:

> But these are written that you may believe that Jesus is the Christ, the Son of God, and that by believing you may have life in his name - **John 20: 31**

Christos is the Greek word for '**Messiah**' and it is used extensively in John's Gospel, but in ways rather different from the Synoptic Gospels. For example, in the Synoptic Gospels, Jesus is secretive about being the Messiah, but in John's Gospel he announces it openly (e.g. **John 4: 26**).

What does it mean to call Jesus 'Christ'?

At the start of John's Gospel, **Andrew** tells his brother Peter that:

> We have found the Messiah - **John 1: 41**

The Fourth Gospel uses the Aramaic word ("*Messian*") for Messiah but the Gospel-writer immediately translates this as "(*that is, the Christ*)" for the benefit of readers unfamiliar with Jewish terms. The fact that the Gospel-writer uses both terms (*Messiah/Christ*) is a clue that the Fourth Gospel will develop its own interpretation of what these words mean that's rooted in Jewish beliefs but isn't entirely the same as them.

> *What you've just read is a good example of **Redaction Criticism**: looking at the choice of words the redactor of John's Gospel makes*

The first chapter of John's Gospel contains several other Messianic titles: "*the one Moses wrote about in the Law, and about whom the Prophets also wrote*", "*Son of God*", "*Son of Man*" and "*King of Israel*". By starting the Gospel this way, John highlights the importance of 'Christ' for understanding who Jesus is.

'Christ' as King

C.H. Dodd argues that, in the Fourth Gospel, the most important meaning of 'Christ' is a **King**. This is why Nathanael calls Jesus the "*King of Israel*" at the start of the Gospel while, at the end of it, Pontius Pilate puts a mocking sign on Jesus' cross calling him "*Jesus of Nazareth, King of the Jews*".

However, the Fourth Gospel never mentions the **line of David** and is not interested in the conventional idea of the **Kingly Messiah**.

- In the middle of the Gospel, straight after the **Feeding of the 5000**, the Galileans try to crown Jesus king, but he escapes them

- When Jesus enters Jerusalem, the crowds greet him singing: "*Blessed is the King of Israel!*" (**John 12: 13**)

- However, days later the crowd demands Jesus is crucified by saying: "*We have no king but Caesar!*" (**John 19: 15**)

- At Jesus' trial, Pilate asks Jesus if he is a king, Jesus replies:

> *My kingdom is not of this world* - **John 18: 36**

The crowds do not see who Jesus truly is: they are expecting the Christ to be a worldly king and they turn on Jesus in anger when he disappoints them. John's Gospel teaches a different sort of meaning of 'Christ'. For John's Gospel, the Christ is a spiritual King who rules over humans' souls, not an earthly king who rules over territory on maps.

This links to the instruction in John's Gospel that believers must be **Born Again**. As physical beings, Christians are the subjects of worldly kings, like the Roman Emperor or Herod; but as creatures who have been spiritually re-born, they have one spiritual King: Christ.

Christ as 'Lamb of God'

C.H. Dodd also argues that 'Christ' can be understood as the **'Lamb of God'**. This is what John the Baptist recognises Jesus as:

> *the Lamb of God, who takes away the sin of the world!* - **John 1: 29**

This phrase is unique to the Fourth Gospel; it doesn't appear in the Synoptics and Jews did not describe the Messiah as being like a Lamb. **Dodd** and **Raymond E. Brown** conclude that the phrase is not something John the Baptist actually said.

> *It fails the **Criterion of Multiple Attestation**, since John the Baptist appears in the Synoptics too but he never uses this phrase there*

The Fourth Gospel clearly links the *Lamb of God* to the Christ because, as soon as John the Baptist calls Jesus the *Lamb of God*, Andrew goes to Peter to announce that they have found the **Messiah**.

The comparison here is with the **Paschal Lamb**. This is the animal sacrificed by the High Priest every Passover Festival in the Jerusalem Temple. This sacrifice commemorates the events in **Exodus 12: 1-28** when the first Paschal Lambs were killed and the blood sprinkled on the door of every Israelite in Egypt so that the Angel of Death would 'pass over' their houses. The Lamb of God is therefore a SACRIFICIAL VICTIM: someone who will die so that others can live. Jesus is the Lamb of God because his death will give believers **Eternal Life**. Just like the Paschal Lamb, Jesus is *"without blemish"* (i.e. sinless).

The Fourth Gospel changes the dating of Jesus' crucifixion to continue this symbolism. In the Synoptic Gospels, Jesus is crucified on the day of Passover (a Friday), but in the Fourth Gospel, Jesus is crucified the day ***before*** Passover (Thursday). This is because the day before Passover is the day the Paschal Lamb is sacrificed: the Gospel presents Jesus dying on the Cross at the same time as the Paschal Lamb dies in the Temple. However, Jesus is the TRUE Lamb of God; the poor animal being killed in the Temple is the substitute.

This is a very different understanding of 'Christ' from the idea of a King and different also from the way the Messiah is viewed in Judaism. It is a distinctively Johannine view of Jesus as the Christ.

Is the purpose of the Fourth Gospel to present Jesus as the Christ?

YES	NO
The Book of Signs begins with Andrew announcing that Jesus is the Messiah and the Book of Glory ends with the promise that readers will have **Eternal Life** if they believe Jesus is the Christ.	The Fourth Gospel presents Jesus as a different sort of Christ from what is expected: a King, but a spiritual king with a spiritual kingdom. The Gospel is trying to change our understanding of what 'Christ' means.
Andrew's announcement follows straight on from John the Baptist's declaration that Jesus is the Lamb of God. This presents Jesus as a sacrificial victim who will die for humanity's sins. This is the true meaning of 'Christ' in Christianity.	This is a very unusual interpretation of Christ. It's not found in the Synoptic Gospels (which link Jesus' suffering instead to the **Suffering Servant in Isaiah 53**). All Christians believe Jesus dies an atoning death, but the idea of Jesus as the Paschal Lamb is unique to the Fourth Gospel.

JESUS AS SON OF GOD

In **John's Gospel**, the 'Book of Signs' concludes with this appeal:

> *But these are written that you may believe that Jesus is the Messiah, the Son of God, and that by believing you may have life in his name* - **John 20: 31**

Moreover, back at the beginning of the Book of Signs, Nathanael declares that Jesus is the "*Son of God*" (**John 1: 49**) so this claim 'bookends' the Fourth Gospel. *Huios Theos* is the Greek phrase for **'Son of God'** which is used in all four Gospels. However, John's Gospel uses this phrase 29 times and speaks of God as 'Father' over 100 times.

What does it mean to call Jesus the 'Son of God'?

In the Old Testament, the phrase *Son of God* can apply to the whole Jewish nation or to a king of Israel. It is a symbolic expression, meaning that the Jewish people are loved by God *as if* they were his children or that a king of Israel *represents* God on Earth by protecting and leading the Jewish people. This is the sense in which Jews expect the **Messiah** to be the *Son of God* - the Messiah will be chosen by God, sent by God to do his work and entrusted with power and responsibility by God, *as if* he were a son, all the while *representing* God to the people on Earth.

The Synoptic Gospels present Jesus as the *Son of God* in a similar way to this Jewish view. In **Mark's Gospel**, Jesus is 'adopted' as God's Son when he is baptized and God's voice announces "*This is my beloved Son*!" However, **Matthew** and **Luke** go further with their birth-narratives: Jesus is announced to be God's Son as soon as he is conceived.

The Fourth Gospel goes furthest of all: Jesus is God's Son since the creation of the universe!

> *This is one of the reasons why the Fourth Gospel doesn't bother with a birth-narrative. Christ existed in the heavenly realm before he appeared on earth. There's no baptism scene because Christ has always been the 'beloved son' of God*

In the Fourth Gospel, Jesus is an eternal being who is present on Earth. He remembers his pre-Earthly existence.

> *I know where I came from and where I am going. But you have no idea where I come from or where I am going* - **John 8: 14**

This Gospel includes ironic jokes about people who do not realise Jesus is the Son of God because they only see a 30 year-old man. When Jesus claims that the ancient patriarch Abraham is delighted with him, the Jewish leaders sneer that Abraham lived centuries ago but Jesus is "*not yet fifty years old*" (**John 8: 57**). Jesus replies with the famous claim:

> *Before Abraham was born, I am!* - **John 8: 58**

> *Yes, this is one of those "I Am" statements the Johannine Jesus is always making.*

Jesus is not just claiming to be very very old (Abraham lived 1500 years previously). Jesus is claiming he comes from outside time altogether: he is eternal. As **C.H. Dodd** says, Jesus belongs "*to a different order of being... outside the range of temporal relations*."

This is a much more unusual idea than being someone God treats *as if* they were a son. **C.H. Dodd** argues that Jesus is on a journey from God to Earth, then from Earth back to God again - and he is taking the people of Earth with him (or at least, all of those who **believe in him**). Those who are united with Christ are 'drawn' by him into his spiritual world of **Eternal Life**.

> *The Johannine Jesus is a divine being on a rescue mission - to rescue humanity!*

Jesus' miraculous **Signs** can be seen as a proof of his heavenly origin. However, the Fourth Gospel places much more emphasis on the idea that Jesus' heavenly origin gives him **insight** into the nature of God. Jesus' whole life reflects what God is like, because Jesus is sent from God.

> *The one who sent me is with me; he has not left me alone, for I always do what pleases him* - **John 8: 29**

Implications

This is a very 'high Christology'. For many traditional Christians, the Fourth Gospel is the one that 'makes sense' of the other Synoptic Gospels. The **revelation** that 'Son of God' means a divine being from outside of time caught on with the wider Christian churches and, by the 2nd century CE, most Christians hold this 'high Christological' view of Jesus as God incarnate.

> *Redaction Critics often point out that the Fourth Gospel has altered the person of Jesus into something pretty far removed from the historical Jesus: that this is not what the original Jesus taught or his disciples believed. However, if the Fourth Gospel really was written by John son of Zebedee, maybe this idea does go back to the original Jesus of Nazareth.*

This sort of belief in 'Son of God' marks a clear break with Judaism, which utterly denies that God can be a human being or a human being can be God. Today there are Unitarian Christians who still reject this sort of interpretation of 'Son of God': they believe that Jesus was inspired by God but they do *not* believe Jesus is God incarnate.

The appeal of the 'high Christological' view is that Jesus is not just a teacher or saviour who lived two thousand years ago; as an eternal being united with God, Jesus is present in your life right now. This means 'believing in Jesus' isn't about holding an opinion concerning a long-dead prophet; it's about forming a relationship with a divine person who is still alive today.

Is the purpose of the Fourth Gospel to present Jesus as the Son of God?

YES	NO
Unlike the Synoptic Gospels, Jesus is openly declared to be the Son of God in John's Gospel: Nathanael says it when he joins Jesus' Disciples and Martha says it before Jesus **raises Lazarus from the dead**.	'Son of God' doesn't mean the same thing in the Fourth Gospel as it (perhaps) means in the Synoptics. The Johannine Jesus is the incarnated Son of God, which is a surprising new idea.
In all the Gospels, Jesus is recognised as the Son of God by some people (such as Peter) - it just happens more often in John's Gospel. In all the Gospels, Jesus represents the ways of God to humanity and forgives sins on behalf of God. In John's Gospel with its **"I Am" statements**, Jesus is just more dramatic about this.	The Synoptic Gospels to varying degrees have an Exaltation Christology, viewing Jesus as a human exalted or adopted to be God's Son. In the Fourth Gospel, Jesus is an eternal being who is present on Earth. He does more than forgive sins: he offers his own **Eternal Life** to people who believe in him (and Christians believe he still does!)

LIFE IN HIS NAME

In **John's Gospel**, the 'Book of Signs' concludes with this appeal:

> But these are written that you may believe that Jesus is the Messiah, the Son of God, and that by believing you may have life in his name - **John 20: 31**

This echoes a promise made in the **Prologue**:

> to those who believed in his name, he gave the right to become children of God - **John 1: 12**

The Gospel is offering a new **Life** to readers who believe in Jesus, but what do they have to do to become **Children of God**? The answer is contained in the phrase "*in His Name*".

How do Christians get Life in His Name?

The Greek language has three words for "**Life**":

- *Bios*, which is physical or biological life

- *Pneuma*, which is mental life or consciousness

- *Zoe*, which is spiritual life

Bios-life is temporary and always runs out in the end. When Jesus **raises Lazarus from the dead**, he restores Lazarus to *Bios*-life, but Lazarus will get sick again and die sooner or later. *Pneuma*-life depends on *Bios*-life: we can't think or feel when our bodies are destroyed or badly damaged. Neither of these types of Life is what the Gospel is referring to.

Zoe-life is different: it is eternal life not just in the sense of being EVERLASTING (it goes on forever) but in the sense of being TIMELESS. The closest we come to *Zoe*-life in ordinary experience is when we are "in the moment" and experience some pleasure deeply and completely in a very fulfilling way. A *Zoe*-life would be like this all the time: deeply fulfilled and engaged with living, appreciative and grateful for everything that comes along, concerned and caring for everyone around you.

> *Traditional Christians regard Zoe-life as both everlasting and timeless- it is a deeply fulfilling way of living and it won't end with death. However, some liberal Christians focus more on the 'timeless' aspect of Zoe-life, perhaps because they don't believe in life after death; some traditional Christians focus more on the 'everlasting' side of things, perhaps because they think earthly life is supposed to be sad and difficult.*

This new type of life can be gained by **believing in Jesus**. This isn't just a matter of agreeing to a bunch of factual statements about Jesus (that he's the Son of God, that he rose from the dead, that he's your Saviour). It's more to do with forming a loving and trusting relationship with Jesus Christ - it's a personal commitment to Jesus.

This is where "*in His Name*" comes into it. Names were very important in Hebrew: they carried power. The holy Name of God was too sacred to pronounce or even write. The Hebrew word for name is *SHEM*, which is linked to the verb meaning "to place". *SHEM* is not just the name that identifies you: it's also your place in the world, your rank or position in the scheme of things.

Because Jesus is the **Son of God** (p46), his name counts as if it was God's Name. This means Jesus has God's authority and power. The Bible **connects** the exaltation of Jesus' Name to his Resurrection:

> *God exalted him to the highest place and gave him the name that is above every name -*
> **Philippians 2: 9**

Jesus has the most exalted name in the universe - the most status, the highest rank

Names can also be "loaned out". For example, a herald might deliver a message 'in the name of the king' and this means that, while he's delivering the message, the herald is in the king's place and has the king's authority and you have to listen respectfully as if it was the king himself speaking. If you tell someone to do something 'in your name', you're telling them you will take responsibility for it: in effect, it counts as if you were doing it, as if they were really you.

So if you act on Jesus' Name, you receive Jesus' status - and his *Zoe*-life that goes with it. But acting on Jesus' Name means acting like Jesus: living your life the way he lived his, which is a life of selflessness, compassionate love and sacrifice for others.

"*Life in His Name*" therefore means a gift of everlasting and/or timeless life, so long as you embody Jesus' Name in your own life, in the things you say and do.

That sounds difficult to do, but fortunately there's help. When you act in the Name of a more powerful person, you get that person's assets added to yours. If you act in a billionaire's name, you get access to his money, so long as you use it for the things he wants. Living in Jesus' Name gives you access to Jesus' spiritual strength. In the Fourth Gospel, Jesus talks about the 'Helper' or 'Comforter' who strengthens believers who do things in his Name: the Greek word is ***PARACLETE***.

> *If you love me, keep my commands, I will ask the Father, and he will give you another*
> *Paraclete to help you and be with you for ever -* **John 14: 15-16**

In this passage, Paraclete *is often translated as 'advocate' (a defender or encourager)*

By the 2nd century, Christians come to regard the *Paraclete* as the **Holy Spirit,** which is the power of God at work in the souls of believers, guiding and strengthening them and answering their prayers.

Implications

The idea of making a commitment to love and follow Jesus and receiving spiritual strength to do this and **Eternal Life** as a reward sounds like a simple recipe for a good religious life. But of course it's often not that simple.

The first Christians regarded a ceremony of baptism as essential to make this commitment to Jesus Christ and receive the Holy Spirit. Many of them experienced exciting SPIRITUAL GIFTS when they did this: prophesying, healing, speaking in tongues. However, over time, conflicts emerged. One of the main ones was what to do about believers who lapsed back into sinful ways after being baptized. Did this mean they were *no longer* living in Jesus' Name because they weren't following his commands? Or did being baptized mean that you were guaranteed Eternal Life *even if* you subsequently sinned?

Some churches ejected members who didn't live up to the high standards of Jesus' Name, whereas others offered multiple chances. Over time, the churches got organised about this. Confessions were introduced so that people could be forgiven for their sins and sins were ranked into venal ones (which could be forgiven) and mortal sins (which couldn't). Christianity developed very strict ethics about sexual behaviour but many of Jesus' warnings about money were taken less seriously.

Reformers have always tried to get back to the exciting offer of a life lived in Jesus' Name. Their churches emphasise religious experiences, being **'Born Again'** and the Gifts of the Spirit during worship; the Holy Spirit is something they experience personally. These days, these Christians refer to themselves as EVANGELICAL.

Other mainstream churches focus on less individualistic worship and following moral rules; the Holy Spirit is something they encounter more indirectly through the Sacraments of Eucharist and Confession.

There's a similar split between whether the Eternal Life the Gospel promises is something that believers will get after they die, or something they are supposed to receive in the here-and-now **C.H. Dodd** calls this second view REALISED ESCHATOLOGY and argues that Jesus taught that Eternal Life was a timeless experience to be enjoyed in the present. Some passages in the Fourth Gospel support this:

> *Whoever hears my word and believes him who sent me has eternal life and will not be judged but has crossed over from death to life* - **John 5: 24**

That sounds like Realised Eschatology; but then the next verse sounds like Future Eschatology:

> *a time is coming when all who are in their graves will hear his voice and come out* - **John 5: 28-29**

Dodd argues that only the first verse represents the *IPSISSIMA VERBA* (the actual words) of Jesus. Most Christians believe that the new Life in Christ is something that is *both* offered in the present *and* consummated in the future - but there's a tendency to focus on one rather than the other.

Is the purpose of John's Gospel to offer believers "Life in Jesus' Name"?

YES	NO
The purpose is clearly stated in the **Prologue** and at the end of the Book of Glory. **Eternal Life is** the main theme of the Fourth Gospel and all Jesus' **Discourses** and **Signs** illustrate the way to get it: not by following the **Law** but by **believing in Jesus** as the **Son of God**.	There turns out to be a catch to this offer: to receive Eternal Life you have to live your life as Jesus lived his, which is to say, perfectly. Jesus' life led him to self-sacrifice and an ugly death. Even if people wanted to live this morally perfect life, most ordinary people can't measure up to it.
Jesus doesn't impose an impossible standard. For one thing, he offers the *Paraclete* or Comforter: his **Holy Spirit** which strengthens the faith of anyone with sincere intentions. Also, Eternal Life brings such a quality to living that it's worth exchanging for mere comfort and prosperity.	The history of the Church shows that living in Jesus' Name isn't as straightforward as it sounds, even with the Comforter helping out. Even if you can deal with backsliders, it's not clear whether Eternal Life refers to the Afterlife or just a better quality experience in THIS lifetime.

SPIRITUAL GOSPEL

Clement of Alexandria (150-215 CE) was a Christian convert who wrote about the origins of the Gospels. Clement argues that **Matthew** was the first Gospel but adds this comment on the Fourth Gospel:

> *But, last of all, John, aware that the physical facts had been set out in the Gospels, was encouraged by his disciples & divinely motivated by the Spirit, composed a spiritual Gospel* - **Clement of Alexandria**

What does Clement mean by calling John "*a spiritual Gospel*"?

In what way is the Fourth Gospel a 'Spiritual Gospel'?

Clement uses the words **Flesh and Spirit** to contrast the other Gospels with **John**. The Synoptics describe Jesus in a fleshy way - in terms of the physical facts - but John goes for the deeper, spiritual meaning behind Jesus' words and actions. Other critics have pointed out that the Synoptics are DESCRIPTIVE but John is REFLECTIVE - or that the Synoptics record *the IPSISSIMA VERBA* (the true words) of Jesus, but John captures the *IPSISSIMA VOX* (the true voice, Jesus' real intentions).

The Protestant reformer **John Calvin** relates Johns Gospel to the Synoptics with this illuminating phrase:

> *This Gospel is the key which opens the door to the understanding of the other Gospels* - **John Calvin**

Martin Luther, the founder of the Protest Reformation, argues that, if some tyrant were to destroy all the books in the Bible, so long as one copy of the Gospel of John survived, "*Christianity would be saved*".

An example of this comes in the **Prologue** with the idea that Christ is the **pre-existent Word of God** who has been active all the way through the Old Testament and participated in the Creation of the World itself. None of the Synoptics comes close to such an exalted view of Jesus - and the author of John's Gospel presumably only developed this understanding over time.

The Fourth Gospel is written in fairly basic Greek. It's not clumsy like **Mark** but it has simple vocabulary and short, direct sentences. However, the everyday concepts in the Fourth Gospel like birth, light, bread and water take on multiple levels of meaning. This is summed up in a very popular quote describing the Gospel:

> *The Gospel of John is like a swimming pool: shallow enough that a child may wade and deep enough that an elephant can swim* – **Leon Morris**

Everyday things become **symbols** of spiritual realities beyond physical sight. Bread becomes a symbol of the spiritual nourishment given by believing in Jesus, who is the **"Bread of Life"**. Water is the symbol of baptism by the Holy Spirit (**John 7:37-39**), to be given to believers when Jesus has been glorified.

In *Topic 2* (*The Person of Jesus*) *you will have studied the* **"I Am" statements** *and the 7 Signs in John's Gospel: these are all good examples of the spiritual depth to the gospel.*

The Fourth Gospel has a distinctive style that draws attention to this spiritual meaning. Jesus makes an claim that can be taken in more than one way.His words carry a spiritual meaning,but he is misunderstood by someone who understands him in a purely earthly way. Jesus then clarifies things. For example, the conversation with **Nicodemus** (**John 3:3-8**) use a Greek word "*anothen*" that may mean "born from above" (Jesus' meaning) or simply "born again" (which is how Nicodemus understands it). Nicodemus simplistically asks how a man can be born a second time without climbing back into his mother's womb? Jesus corrects him:

> *No one can enter the kingdom of God unless they are born of water and the Spirit* - **John 3: 5**

Jesus adds that **flesh** (*sarx*) gives birth to flesh, but the **Spirit** (*pneuma*) gives birth to Spirit. Very simple words are being used here (birth, water, spirit, flesh), but the meaning involves baptism with water into a **new eternal life in Jesus' Name** (p51).

Implications

The apparent simplicity of John's Gospel makes it the most popular Gospel in polls of church-goers. However, this simplicity of language disguises layer upon layer of symbols and codes and some deeply mysterious insights into the nature of God and faith. John's LANGUAGE may be simple but his MEANING is not.

This spiritual depth has allowed some readers to get quite carried away. In the 2nd century, the Johannine churches were split between Christians who took a conventional view of the meaning of the Gospel and those who read a completely different set of meanings into it. These were the **Gnostics**, who believed that a secret wisdom (in Greek, *gnosis*) was coded into the Fourth Gospel. The Gnostics concluded that spiritual realities were the only thing that mattered, that the physical world was evil and that Jesus had been a spirit-being who only *appeared* to be human

Raymond E. Brown calls these people "secessionists" (meaning 'splitters' who broke away from the church's teachings) and thinks that their beliefs were "*a plausible exaggeration... of certain features of the Fourth Gospel*". In other words, they took the Gospel's talk of being Born from the Spirit and receiving **Eternal Life** to an extreme conclusion. The New Testament contains 3 **epistles** (letters) supposedly written by 'John' that condemn these splitters and argue for the correct interpretation of the Fourth Gospel.

Most scholars don't think these letters were written by the same **John** who is supposed to have written the Fourth Gospel - and certainly not by the **Beloved Disciple** (p42). They are from the 2nd century and not even **John son of Zebedee** (p41) lived that long. But they are clearly from the same **Johannine Community** (p43) that created the Fourth Gospel and they are still wrestling with the same electrifying spiritual themes the Gospel raises.

These themes continue to excite and trouble Christian communities today. John's Gospel suggests a powerful inner transformation is needed for the believer to understand spiritual realities. There are many people who claim to have experienced this transformation and they offer to teach the secrets to followers. This is how cults form. The mainstream churches have always guarded against cults and people claiming to have secret spiritual wisdom, but sometimes they go too far and resist genuine spiritual insights and calls to reform corrupt practices. John's Gospel offers a vision of Christian living as more mysterious, exciting and transformative than just 'going to church' every Sunday, but Christians have not found it easy to put its ideas into practice.

Is the Fourth Gospel intended to be "a spiritual Gospel"?

YES	NO
The **Prologue** begins with a spiritual power from outside of time and space coming into our world. All the way through, Jesus insists that behind our ordinary objects and activities (eating, drinking, washing) are spiritual realities waiting to transform us. The Gospel encourages us to see the world with new eyes, which is what being 'Born Again' means.	These 'spiritual realities' are very vague: people seem to find whatever they want in John's Gospel. The Gnostic interpretation is just as valid as the Johannine Church's official interpretation. John's Gospel is best when it avoids these muddles and focuses on its key message of Christians loving one another. The spiritual symbolism is a distraction.
John's Gospel emphasises that there is more to the Christian life than good deeds and regular worship. It encourages Christians to seek transformative religious experiences and become united with God through Christ in a much deeper sense. The **Eternal Life** offered by John's Gospel is a transformed way of living in the world today.	The Synoptic Gospels also call for people to live their lives in a transformed way, although they call it 'repentance' rather than being Born Again. **C.H. Dodd** claims that Realised Eschatology is present in Luke's Parables just as much as John's Signs. John's Gospel differs in style from the Synoptics but not in its main message about believing in Christ.

THE FULFILLMENT OF SCRIPTURE

Matthew's Gospel uses **proof-texts** to link Jesus to prophecies about the **Messiah** in the Old Testament, but **John's Gospel** is just as concerned about fulfilling Old Testament prophecies, even though it isn't quite so explicit about it.

How does Jesus fulfill the Scriptures in the Fourth Gospel?

The Fourth Gospel presents Jesus Christ as the **Messiah** that the Old Testament predicted hundreds of years previously. **Isaiah 53** features the **Suffering Servant** who is tortured by the very people he tries to help. The Fourth Gospel refers to this at the beginning:

> *He came to that which was his own, but his own did not receive him* - **John 1: 11**

Isaiah 9:6 describes the Messiah as ruling over an eternal and everlasting kingdom. The Fourth Gospel presents Jesus as divine and existing eternally. All of Jesus' **"I Am" statements** imply this, but when he declares *"Before Abraham was born, I am"*, Jesus makes it explicit that he is the eternal **Son of God**.

Isaiah 53: 4–6 explains that this **Suffering Servant** would die in the place of his people. In the Fourth Gospel, the High Priest Caiaphas urges the death penalty for Jesus saying that *"one man dies for the people"* (**John 11: 50**) which fulfils the prophecy.

The Fourth Gospel crafts the story of the Crucifixion to show many prophecies being fulfilled, such as:

> *a pack of villains encircles me; they pierce my hands and my feet* - **Psalm 22: 16**

This is fulfilled when Jesus is crucified between two outlaws:

> *they crucified him, and with him two others – one on each side and Jesus in the middle* - **John 19: 18**

While he is dying, Jesus' clothes are divided up between his executioners; finding the cloth to be seamless, the soldiers throw dice to see who gets it:

> *They divide my clothes among them and cast lots for my garment* - **Psalm 22: 18**

After Jesus dies, a soldier checks he is dead by stabbing him in the ribs with a spear while Jesus' mother watches on:

> *They will look on me, the one they have pierced, and they will mourn for him as one mourns for an only child* - **Zechariah 12: 10**

However, unlike the other executed victims, Jesus' bones are not broken. This fulfils the instruction in **Exodus 12: 46** for preparing the **Paschal Lamb** (the animal sacrificed at Passover), that none of the bones should be broken.

Implications

Redaction Critics point out that the **Johannine Community** (p43) experienced a lot of conflict with the Jewish Synagogues over whether or not Jesus was the Messiah. As a result, the Fourth Gospel has been carefully crafted to support the Johannine Community's position. Some Critics might suggest that the Gospel-writer has added details that weren't historical just to get a 'match' with an Old Testament prophecy.

> *However, if we apply the **Criterion of Multiple Attestation**, then the dividing up of Jesus' clothes is also described in **Matthew 27: 35**, so this may be a historical detail*

The fulfillment of prophecy is important because it supports the argument that the entirety of the Old Testament and the Law was both inspired **by** Jesus (as the **Logos**) and is also **about** Jesus. Everything that happens in the Old Testament, from Moses meeting God in the burning bush through to King David's unhappy family life and the Babylonian Exile, it's all supposed to prepare the Jews to recognise the **Christ** when he appears. The irony is that they don't.

It's important in another sense, because it shows that God is in control of history. It often appears to humans that God is not in control and that the power of evil - the Darkness - rules the world. The Fourth Gospel begins by proclaiming that the **Darkness** can never overcome the **Light** and demonstrates this by showing how every detail of Jesus' suffering fits into a plan laid down by God in the Scriptures hundreds of years before.

Is the purpose of the Fourth Gospel to show how Jesus fulfils Scripture?

YES	NO
In the **Prologue**, the Gospel refers to the **Suffering Servant** and the Crucifixion scene contains multiple references to the Psalms, the Prophets and the Paschal Lamb. This shows that Jesus is the source and also the subject matter of the Scriptures.	**Redaction Criticism** would say that the whole of the Fourth Gospel has been crafted precisely to provide 'ammunition' for the arguments between the **Johannine Community** and the Jewish Synagogues that have rejected them. We can't be sure these details are historical.
The way that Scriptures are fulfilled despite (or even because of) the plots of evil men shows that God is completely in control of history. Even when the evildoers think they have the righteous man at their mercy, they are only acting out a script created by God centuries before.	This has troubling implications for **freewill** and **God's goodness**. If God created these prophecies, does it mean that people like Judas, Pilate and Caiaphas have no freewill? And why would a good God choose a plan that involves so much unnecessary suffering?

A GOSPEL TO CONVERT JEWS & GENTILES

Who was the intended audience of the Fourth Gospel: who was it written **for**? There are two main answers:

- it is aimed at **Jewish readers**, trying to persuade them that Jesus is the **Messiah**

- it is aimed at Gentiles (non-Jews), trying to persuade them that Christ's offer of **Eternal Life** is for them too.

Christianity began as a messianic sect within Judaism and could have stayed that way. However, it became a MISSIONARY RELIGION, because Christians set out to convert other people to their faith.

The Gospels present this as a commandment from the Risen Christ, which is known as the **'Great Commission'** in Matthew's Gospel (**Matthew 28: 19**). A version of this appears in the **Fourth Gospel** at the end of the Book of Glory:

> *As the Father has sent me, so I send you* - **John 20: 21**

> *You might remember the **Sign of Healing the Blind Man**, which involved going to a pool called Siloam ('sent'). The idea of being 'sent' by God is a theme in John's Gospel and it always ends in the **Word of God** being proclaimed.*

Christians call trying to persuade others to convert to their faith EVANGELISM and the four Gospel-writers are often referred to as the EVANGELISTS because their writings are intended to persuade non-believers that Jesus is **Christ** and the **Son of God**.

Argument: Converting Jews

On first reading, the Fourth Gospel is aimed at converting Jewish readers to Christianity. The Gospel starts with an imitation of the **Book of Genesis** - its opening words are *"in the beginning..."* which are the same words that begin Genesis. In fact, the Book of Genesis is named *BERESHIT* in Hebrew, which simply means "In the Beginning".

The first person to become a Disciple of Jesus is Andrew who tells his brother Peter that, *"We have found the Messiah"* (**John 1: 41**). The Gospel here uses the Aramaic word *Messian* rather than the Greek word *Christos*, which emphasises its Jewish credentials.

More than this, the whole of the Fourth Gospel is taken up with debates between Jesus and Jewish leaders: first of all **Nicodemus**, then the **Pharisees** and priests and finally the High Priest **Caiaphas**. In these discussions, Jesus corrects the Jews' beliefs about God and the **Jewish Law**. The Gospel-writer refers to many specific places in Jerusalem and often knows about Jewish feasts and traditions. Jesus' actions often correspond to Jewish festivals, such as Jesus' **"I Am the Light of the World"** Discourse occurring during the Feast of Tabernacles, when the Temple was lit up. A lot of the conflict in the Gospel is over how to keep the Sabbath regulations (for example, in the **Sign of the Healing of the Blind Man**).

However...

The Fourth Gospel doesn't read like something that would be very persuasive to a Jewish reader. Jesus' enemies are referred to as "*the Jews*" even by the Disciples themselves and Jesus refers to "*your Law*" as if he isn't a Jew either. More than that, the Jews are called *children of the Devil* (**John 8: 44**) and presented as murderers and hypocrites.

> *It's possible these insults are only meant for the leaders of the Jews, not ordinary Jewish believers, but it's still a strange way to try to persuade someone*

There's also the problem of the 'high Christology' in the Gospel that would be offensive to many Jews. Jesus links himself with God when he says, "*before Abraham was born, I am*" (**John 8: 58**) and this is a blasphemous idea for Jews. Possibly even more disgusting to a Jewish reader would be Jesus saying:

> *Whoever eats my flesh and drinks my blood remains in me, and I in them* - **John 6: 56**

Jesus is referring to the **EUCHARIST** where Christians share bread and wine, but a Jewish reader would probably not know that. They *would* know that eating anything with blood in it is completely forbidden in Judaism.

> *In short, it's hard to imagine a worse Gospel for trying to convert Jews to Christianity -* ***Matthew*** *would work much better.*

Argument: Converting Gentiles

An alternative argument is that the Fourth Gospel is aimed at a Gentile audience, persuading them to give up their pagan ways and convert to Christianity. There was certainly an audience for this sort of message in the 1st and 2nd centuries CE; many Roman pagans attended Synagogues to learn more about God, but were put off becoming Jews because of the extensive Laws (and of course, circumcision for men). They were referred to as *metuentes* ('God-fearers').

The Fourth Gospel would have an appeal for this audience. It presents Jesus in **Hellenic** terms, using concepts from Greek philosophy like the **Logos**. It also uses universal symbolism of **light and darkness**, **flesh and spirit**, bread, water and birth. Many of these Gentiles were **DUALISTS** who would have been interested in these symbols of two worlds: a physical world we can see and a heaven world we cannot see. The concept of **Jesus as the Son of God** would not have been offensive to pagans.

Jesus also rejects many of the details of the Jewish Law, which would have appealed to Gentiles since this was off-putting for them in Judaism. Instead, Jesus offers spiritual re-birth and **Eternal Life** without complicated rituals or surgical operations - very attractive.

However...

Gentiles don't feature much in the Fourth Gospel. **Matthew's Gospel** goes out of its way to present many Gentiles as recognising Christ while the Jews don't (e.g. the **Magi visit Jesus after he is born**). **Luke's Gospel** presents Jesus as offering a universal message to all people, Jewish and Gentile alike. But in the Fourth Gospel, Jesus spends most of his time arguing with Jewish leaders. He does visit the Samaritans and convert them - but to pagan Gentiles, the Samaritans would have looked like just another type of Jew. The specific details about Jerusalem and Jewish festivals would have been off-putting (or incomprehensible) to a Gentile reader.

Argument: Converting Crypto-Christians & followers of John the Baptist

Raymond E. Brown offers a different solution: an audience of *"crypto-Christians"*.

'Crypto-' means 'secret'. These people were Jews in the local Synagogues who were secret Christians (or at least, who believed Jesus was the **Messiah**).

Brown argues that, when the **Johannine Community** (p43) was expelled from the Synagogues after 90 CE, they left behind many friends and family members who secretly shared their faith but who didn't have the courage to stand up for their beliefs and take the consequences. These people kept quiet when the Christians were expelled, but they were sympathetic to Christianity and just needed a 'push' to 'come out' as believers in Christ.

The Fourth Gospel seems to refer to these crypto-Christians when it says:

> *They would not openly acknowledge their faith for fear they would be put out of the synagogue* - **John 12: 42**

> *The crypto-Christians perhaps agreed with criticisms of the Jewish Law, would have known that the Eucharist didn't really involve blood-drinking but just needed persuading that Jesus was the **Son of God**.*

Brown also speculates that a Jewish sect following **John the Baptist** was still in existence in the late 1st century CE. These Baptizers would perhaps have been hostile to the Pharisees too, but not willing to admit that Jesus of Nazareth was greater than John the Baptist. The Fourth Gospel tries to win them over by presenting John in a positive way, but making it clear that Jesus, not John, is the true **Light** from God.

Can we work out the intended audience of the Fourth Gospel?

YES	NO
The Fourth Gospel contains such specific details about Jewish festivals and laws as well as a precision about Judean geography, it must surely have been written for a Jewish audience who would understand these references.	The Gospel is too hostile to Jews to be for a Jewish audience unconvinced by the claim the Jesus is the Christ. However, it's too Jewish-focused to be aimed at Gentiles, who would not pick up on these references or care about the arguments over Sabbath rules, Moses or Abraham.
The Fourth Gospel doesn't make a serious attempt to win over hostile Jewish readers and doesn't show much interest in Gentiles (other than Samaritans). Brown's argument that the Gospel was aimed at an audience of 'crypto-Christians' fits the best.	Since we don't know for sure who wrote the Gospel, or where, or when, any attempt to work out its audience is futile. The Gospel addresses itself to one audience: YOU, the current reader, who is invited to believe in **Jesus as the Son of God** and receive **Life in His Name**.

KEY SCHOLARS

Raymond E Brown

Topic: 3.2 Purpose & Authorship of the Fourth Gospel

Raymond E Brown (1928-1998) is an American Roman Catholic priest and Bible scholar whose work features in other topics in this course too **(1.1 Prophecy regarding the Messiah, 2.2 Titles of Jesus, 2.3 Miracles & Signs)**.

Brown carries on the work on John's Gospel started by **C.H. Dodd**. In *The Gospel & the Epistles of John: A Concise Commentary* (1988), Brown goes through John's Gospel passage-by-passage, exploring the terminology and the symbolism. Brown follows Dodd's concept of 'realised eschatology' – he thinks Jesus' acts and words reveal timeless truths about life and God rather than predicting things that are going to happen after death or at the end of time.

In *The Community of the Beloved Disciple* (1979), Brown explores the **Johannine Community** and how its situation influences the way John's Gospel presents Jesus. The subtitle of the book is *The Life, Loves and Hates of an Individual Church in New Testament Times*. Notice the word "Hates": Brown focuses on the deep rift between the Johannine Christians and the Jewish Synagogues that expelled them in the 80s and 90s CE.

Brown didn't discover the idea of the Johannine Community. **J. Louis Martyn** was the first to develop this concept, but Brown references Martyn in his book and builds on his scholarship.

Brown argues that the Johannine Christians experienced a deep trauma when they were expelled from the Jewish religion. Not only did they lose friends and family, but they were exposed to danger. Now that they were no longer Jews, they were expected by the Roman authorities to join in pagan sacrifices. Those that refused were arrested and even executed. Brown suspects that the Jewish leaders sometimes informed on these Christians. This explains the 'Hate' towards "*the Jews*" and what he calls "*the deep sense of 'us' against 'them'*" in John's Gospel.

Brown also suggests that the entirety of John's Gospel tells a coded story of the Johannine Community's experiences and the development of their faith. Brown thinks the Johannine Community was founded by Jewish followers of John the Baptist who came to believe Jesus was the Messiah. They came under pressure from the Jewish leaders for their beliefs and developed a higher Christology when they were joined by Samaritan converts. Eventually, they were expelled from the Synagogue in the 80s or early 90s CE. Brown believes they wrote the Fourth Gospel to appeal to "*crypto-Christians*" in the Jewish community who concealed their faith in Jesus.

Brown believes that the Beloved Disciple was a real person: not John son of Zebedee nor a member of Jesus' Twelve Disciples, but an actual follower of Jesus who preserved some eyewitness memories of Jesus and some distinctive beliefs about him. The Fourth Gospel was written in its final form after this Beloved Disciple died.

C.H. Dodd

Topic: 3.1 Purpose & authorship of the Fourth Gospel

Charles Harold Dodd (1884-1973) is an Welsh Protestant Bible scholar whose work features in other topics in this course too **(2.1 (Prologue in John), 2.2 (Titles of Jesus in the Synoptics and selected 'I Am' sayings in John), 2.3 (Miracles and Signs))**.

Dodd is a very influential figure in Bible scholarship. His work argues against the conclusions drawn by **Albert Schweitzer** and **Rudolph Bultmann**. Both of these scholars tried to analyse the Bible to uncover the historical Jesus by stripping away the supernatural elements. They concluded that Jesus was a rather murky historical figure whose political and religious ambitions were pretty remote from modern life. Dodd argues against this, saying that we can reconstruct details about Jesus' teachings and these are relevant to people in the modern world.

Dodd wrote two books relevant to this part of the course. ***The Interpretation of the Fourth Gospel*** (1953) goes through all John's key concepts and analyses them in terms of their link to the Old Testament or Hellenic philosophy. It's a dense read because Dodd is the sort of scholar who writes 'Logos' as λογοσ and expects you to know your Greek alphabet well enough to understand.

Historical Tradition in the Fourth Gospel (1963) is a little more accessible. Dodd argues that the author of Johns Gospel is a '*historian*' and not a '*chronicler*'. In other words, the author of the Fourth Gospel is interested in the meaning of historical events and freely edits and alters stories and puts speeches into characters' mouths to draw out this meaning. However, Dodd does think there are historical details in the Gospel and that they can be reconstructed by scholars.

Dodd's main contribution is the idea of REALISED ESCHATOLOGY. 'Eschatology' is philosophy about the 'End Times' (from the Greek, *Eschaton*) such as death, Judgement Day and the Afterlife. A typical Jewish eschatology among the Pharisees in the 1st century was that at some point in the future, God would send his Messiah to begin the Messianic Age where God would rule the world, abolishing sin and suffering.

According to Dodd, Jesus taught a 'realised eschatology', that these End Times were ***already happening***. This means that Bible passages Heaven, Hell, Judgement Day etc should be interpreted symbolically as religious experiences Christians have in the present.

Dodd's views are popular with Liberal Christians, because they involve focusing on the spiritual meaning of the Bible rather than predictions about the end of the world, the threat of damnation in Hell or a focus on going to Heaven after you die. These views are unpopular with Conservative Christians who prefer to take the supernatural elements in the Bible more literally and have a 'futurist eschatology' (Judgement Day is coming in the future).

GLOSSARY OF TERMS

Apocalypticism: Belief in the coming end of the world

Apocrypha: Books that were not included in the Biblical **canon**; non-canonical books

Beloved Disciple: Mysterious figure who appears from chapter 13 of John's Gospel; may represent the author of John's Gospel

Canon: The officially recognised list of books in the Bible; considered to be inspired by God; Scripture

Christology: Theory about the status of Christ, from an **exalted** human (low Christology) to an **incarnated** divine being (high Christology)

Conservatism: Christian trend opposed to **liberalism** and trying to conserve Biblical truths; see **traditionalism**

Crypto-Christians: Jewish Christians who concealed their faith to avid expulsion from the Synagogues after 90 CE

Enlightenment: Period from mid 17th to late 18th century when European scholars pioneered a new scientific outlook

Exaltation: Promotion of a human to a divine rank

Form Criticism: Interpretation of the Bible based on its origins as *pericopae* circulating among the first Christian communities

Fourth Gospel: Another term for John's Gospel

Incarnation: Arrival of a divine being in physical form

Jewish Revolt: Rebellion against Rome 67-73 CE, resulting in the destruction of the Temple in 70 CE

Johannine Community: Community of Jewish and Samaritan Christians who were expelled from the Synagogues, perhaps in Antioch c. 90 CE; composed John's Gospel

John the Baptist: Figure mentioned in all the Gospels who preceded Jesus and baptized many followers but was executed by Herod Antipas

Kerygma: Greek for 'preaching'; the original Christian message of Jesus and his Apostles

Liberal Christianity: Christian trend opposed to **conservatism** and freely interpreting the Bible to new circumstances

Logia: Sayings of Jesus passed on by his followers as part of the **oral tradition**

Markan Priority: Theory that Mark is the earliest Gospel and was copied by Matthew and Luke

Modernism: Christian trend opposed to **traditionalism** that redefines Christian teachings for the modern world

Oral Tradition: Accounts of Jesus memorized and passed on by word-of-mouth before the Gospels came to be written

Pericope: In **Form Criticism**, a textual unit that was original a memory of Jesus passed on by word of mouth before the Gospels were written (plural *pericopae*)

Pharisees: Jewish sect concerned with obeying the Law in every aspect of life; represented as in conflict with the first Christians

Prologue: The introduction to a Gospel

Proto-Gospel: Theoretical early Gospel which is now lost but was the basis for the Synoptic Gospels

Q-Source: Theoretical source for material common to Matthew and Luke that is not shared by Mark; from German *Quelle* ('source')

Redaction Criticism: Interpretation of the Bible based on the idea of a redactor editing earlier material to address issues going on in the church in his time

Sitz im Leben: 'Life Situation'; the context in which the *pericopae* were first composed, according to **Form Criticism**

Source Criticism: Interpretation of the Bible based on the different sources each Gospel is composed of

Synagogue: Local prayer house and centre of Jewish worship after the **Jewish Revolt**

Synoptic Gospel: Matthew, Mark and Luke; from the Greek 'seen together' because of the shared content and structure of these Gospels

Synoptic Problem: The problem of explaining the similarities and differences between the **Synoptic Gospels**

Traditionalism: Christian trend opposed to **modernism** that resists redefining Christian teachings for the modern world

ABOUT THE AUTHOR

Jonathan Rowe is a teacher of Religious Studies, Psychology and Sociology at Spalding Grammar School and he creates and maintains the **www.psychologywizard.net** site for Edexcel A-Level Psychology. He has worked as an examiner for various Exam Boards but is not affiliated with Edexcel. This series of books grew out of the resources he created for his students. Jonathan also writes novels and creates resources for his hobby of fantasy wargaming. He likes warm beer and smooth jazz.

Printed in Great Britain
by Amazon